The
HARVEST
collection

Eighty delicious dishes without meat

Evans

GARDNER MERCHANT

 Trusthouse Forte

Published by Evans Brothers Limited
2A Portman Mansions
Chiltern Street
London W1M 1LE

First published 1990
Typeset by Fleetlines Typesetters
Printed by New Interlitho S.p.A., Milan

ISBN 0 237 51193 2

ACKNOWLEDGEMENTS
The original idea for this book developed from a project undertaken by the Management Trainees of the Educational Services Division of Gardner Merchant.
The following people in the organization have worked together to produce this collection of vegetarian recipes:
Peter Howell
Divisional Director
Peter Hazzard
Food Services and Training Director
Julia Lloyd
Food Services Development Manager
Stephen Pini
Executive Chef and Craft Training Manager
Anne Simpson
Chief Dietitian

All crockery was supplied by Lockhart Catering Equipment
Photography by Ivor Innes
Designed by Neil Sayer
Edited by Alison Leach

Contents

Foreword

As an international organization, we serve over a million meals every day. This gives us an excellent opportunity of recognizing trends in eating patterns. Recently we have seen a significant increase in the popularity of the vegetarian dishes offered on our menus. Research has shown us that this does not mean a phenomenal growth of vegetarians among our customers but it certainly reveals the growing number of those who may be termed demi-vegetarians – people who prefer to eat less meat, fish and poultry.

The eighty mouth-watering recipes in this collection have been specially created by our highly skilled chefs and cooks for you to enjoy making for your family and friends.
Bon appetit!

Garry Hawkes
Managing Director – Gardner Merchant Limited

On her visit to Gardner Merchant's International Training Centre, HRH the Princess Royal accepted a cheque for £200,000 on behalf of Save the Children.

For each copy of this book that is sold Gardner Merchant will make a contribution towards a target of £10,000 for Save the Children.

Introduction

Designed to appeal to vegetarians and demi-vegetarians alike, this collection of recipes is far removed from the traditional image of vegetarian food being stodgy and dull. It shows how light, imaginative and appetizing it can be.

A selection of recipes has been made for each of the four seasons – spring, summer, autumn and winter – all emphasizing the potential of vegetarian cooking. Most of the recipes contain suggestions for variations, thus greatly extending the number of dishes for you to try.

A healthy, well-balanced diet is of course very important for everyone and this was carefully considered in choosing the recipes. Guidelines are given on how to achieve this simply and each recipe is graded in terms of its protein, fat and fibre contents. Semi-skimmed milk, low-fat cheeses, polyunsaturated fats and wholemeal flour are recommended as ingredients (where applicable).

Many people are still rather confused by the range of beans and pulses that are now available in both supermarkets and health food shops. The use of the different types is simplified by the inclusion of a table setting out the exact preparation and cooking methods.

Vegetarian food is sometimes accused of being bland. The recipes will show you how the less pronounced flavours of beans and lentils can easily be enhanced by the subtle use of herbs, spices and accompanying sauces. Whenever possible, use fresh herbs; many varieties can be grown successfully in pots on a sunny windowsill or patio.

The colour photographs of each dish show how important the presentation is in making food look tempting. The garnishes are relatively simple and quick to make – they are, however, merely suggestions to stimulate your imagination. Even if you do not always have the time when making a dish for the family to add any garnish, try to do so when you are entertaining. Many of the recipes are ideal for introducing your friends to a healthier eating pattern – even those who have previously dismissed vegetarian dishes will be converted once they have tasted some of the gourmet treats in this book.

Many dishes are enhanced by an accompanying sauce; the recipes on pages 96–98 show how to make these taste wonderful without resorting to cream.

Apart from the recipes, you will find much invaluable information in this book. You may, for example, have to make sandwiches regularly and be in need of new ideas for fillings. From the thirty suggestions given on pages 100 and 101 you are certain to discover some combinations that will appeal to you. You will also find that the collection of culinary tips on page 5 will help you to achieve perfect results when following the recipes.

The Harvest Collection will certainly prove an indispensable source of inspiration to every health-conscious cook.

Unless otherwise stated each recipe serves 4.

Nutritional Analysis

For a healthy, well-balanced vegetarian diet it is important to consider the protein, fat and fibre content of any dish. *The Harvest Collection* offers an insight to the nutritional balance of each recipe.

It is recommended that a balanced vegetarian diet should have sufficient protein and be low in fat and high in fibre. You will find some of the dishes included in this collection are high in fat, some low in protein and others low in fibre. By choosing complementary dishes to eat at this meal, you can adjust the balance as necessary. *It must be emphasized that the analyses were calculated on the given ingredients; any variation will make the relevant analysis invalid.*

Protein

It is recommended that 13 percent of our total calories each day should come from protein. For someone consuming 2000 calories per day, this is the equivalent of 22 g protein eaten at each of the three meals. A meat eater would easily obtain 28 g protein from a 100 g (4 oz) portion of meat. Vegetarians, however, need to plan the entire meal carefully to ensure a good intake of protein. If the main dish is low in protein, choose complementary items with a high-protein level.

High-protein foods include soya products, beans, pulses, wholegrains and seeds. Milk and cheese are also rich in protein but should be eaten in moderation because of their high level of saturated fat. Semi-skimmed milk and low-fat cheeses are a healthier choice. Good sources of protein for vegetarians are:

Grains wholegrain: bread, pasta, rice, breakfast cereals, oats, rye and barley

Nuts and Seeds cashews, hazelnuts, almonds, peanuts, sunflower seeds, sesame seeds

Pulses and Beans dried beans (eg: kidney, butter and haricot), lentils, chickpeas

Fat

It is recommended that 35 percent or less of our total daily calories comes from fat. Most of us eat more than this. A balanced diet should contain some fat and the occasional high-fat dish is not harmful, provided it is complemented by low-fat dishes. It is the overall balance over a period of time that is important, rather than a dish-by-dish or even meal-by-meal assessment.

Cholesterol

If you are concerned about your blood cholesterol levels, you should take care not to eat too much fat, particularly saturated fat. It is the total fat in your diet which can lead to a raised blood cholesterol level.

Fibre

The recommended intake is 30 g of fibre per day. This is not difficult to achieve when you realize that on average one piece of fresh fruit contains 4 g and one slice of wholemeal bread 3 g. A diet high in fibre is considered to be beneficial to general health. A vegetarian diet naturally provides a high-fibre intake with its extensive use of fresh vegetables, wholemeal flours, grains and pulses.

All these facts and figures may be difficult to absorb, so each recipe in this book has been analysed for protein, fat and fibre and then given a grading of high, medium or low. These gradings are based on the UK recommendations at the time of publication. The analyses relate to one portion based on the recommended portion yield from the relevant recipes.

	High	**Medium**	**Low**
Protein	17 g or more	12–16 g	0–11 g
Fat	18 g or more	6–17 g	0–5 g
Fibre	8 g or more	4–7g	0–3 g

Cooking Pulses and Beans

Pulses and beans are important ingredients in vegetarian cookery being good sources of protein and fibre but low in fat. Beans have an in-built protection system to prevent their being taken by 'wildlife' in their natural environment. It is for this reason that they must be handled correctly before being used in recipes.

Wash dried pulses or beans two or three times in fresh cold water, then drain. Cover with twice their volume of fresh cold water and leave to soak for a minimum of 4 hours or preferably overnight. Drain.

Put the pulses or beans in a pan and cover with fresh cold water, bring to the boil and boil rapidly for 10 minutes. Reduce the heat, cover the pan and simmer until tender. (Actual cooking times shown in table.) If a pulse or bean is cooked, it should squash easily when pressed. Lentils will form a pulp-like mixture.

Do not add salt, vinegar, lemon juice or any sauce or dressing until the pulses or beans are cooked; otherwise you will find that their skins will toughen.

A pressure cooker can be used which will considerably reduce the cooking times. Consult the manufacturer's instruction booklet for details.

A number of the recipes in this book contain various types of pulses and beans. All can be bought dried and the table below gives instructions as to the preparation and cooking requirements of each one after initial boiling. If these seem too time-consuming, the majority are also widely available canned.

PULSE/BEAN	DESCRIPTION	PREPARATION	AVERAGE COOKING TIME
ADUKI BEANS	Small red beans with a sweet nutty taste; ideal addition to soups, stews, curries, salads and rice	Soak overnight	40 minutes
BLACK-EYE BEANS	Round white beans distinguished by a black mark on one side; use in soups, salads, rice dishes and casseroles	Soak overnight	45–50 minutes
BLACK BEANS	Shiny black beans mainly used for sprouting; use whole in savoury dishes	Soak overnight	50–60 minutes
BROAD BEANS	Large flat brown beans, also known as haba or horse bean; use in stews and casseroles	Soak overnight	1½ hours
BUTTER BEANS	Also known as lima beans, with a slightly sweet taste; blend well with most dishes	Soak overnight	1–1½ hours

CANNELLINI BEANS	Creamy whole kidney beans with a light texture	Soak overnight	45–50 minutes
CHICKPEAS	High in protein, a versatile pulse with a unique taste, also known as garbanzo peas; use in falafel, hummus or can be added to most main courses and salads	Soak overnight	1–1½ hours
FLAGEOLET BEANS	Pale green beans usually cooked and puréed, eg pease pudding	Soak overnight	40–45 minutes
FUL MEDAME BEANS	Small brown beans with thick skins and earthy taste; use in soups and stews	Soak overnight	55–60 minutes
GREEN PEAS	Whole: pale green wrinkled skin; use in stews and hotpots. Split: usually cooked and puréed for eating as a vegetable	Soak overnight. Soaking improves texture but can be cooked without	1–1½ hours 30 minutes
HARICOT BEANS	Better known as baked beans, very high in protein and extremely versatile	Soak overnight	1½ hours
LENTILS	Vary in colour from green, orange pink to brown, the most common being red; a valuable source of protein; use in a variety of dishes	Soaking is not necessary for red lentils; a short soaking period improves texture of other types	Red lentils 20 minutes Others 45 minutes
MUNG BEANS	Range in colour from green through yellow to golden and black; olive green variety usually used for sprouting	Soak overnight	30–45 minutes
PINTO BEANS	A variety of haricot bean with a mottled brown skin which changes to pink when cooked	Soak overnight	1–1½ hours
RED KIDNEY BEANS	Plump, red and shiny; a classic ingredient in Mexican cooking but will add colour and taste to most dishes	Soak overnight (essential)	1 hour
SOYA BEANS	Very valuable source of protein, after cooking can be used in many foods; also available in commercial products, eg: soya milk, tofu, soy sauce and soya flour	Soak overnight	3 hours

Culinary Tips

This collection of tips, compiled during the testing of the recipes, will help you to achieve perfect results.

Remember always to use vegetable stock in all vegetarian recipes. Dilute one vegetable stock cube with 13 fl oz/400 ml of water or crumble the cube as specified in the recipes.

For recipes that involve stuffing peppers, always blanch the pepper first. The best method is to slice off the base thinly to allow the water to penetrate inside. Dip the pepper in boiling water for 1–2 minutes, remove and refresh. Slice off the top of the 'lid' and reserve. Remove the seeds and discard.

In making hot yogurt sauce, use half yogurt, half Béchamel; this will help to prevent the yogurt from separating.

Where wholemeal flour is given in recipes, a mixture of 50 percent wholemeal flour and 50 percent white flour may be used to give a lighter texture. To enhance the appearance and quality of a dish, white sauces have been prepared with white flour.

The use of fresh herbs is recommended – you will find that their delicate flavours greatly improve a dish. If they are unavailable, dried herbs can be used but the quantities given in the recipes should be halved.

To make a bread basket for garnish, mould a triangle of bread into a suitable round container such as a dariole mould. Put in a cool oven and bake until dry. Remove the basket, allow to cool and use as described.

To make filo pastry baskets, cut filo pastry into three 2-in/5-cm squares. Grease the outside of a dariole mould, lay one layer of filo on top and brush with water. Place a second layer of filo on top and brush with water; repeat with a third layer. Put the mould upside-down in the oven and bake at 400°F/200°C/gas mark 6 until golden, about 5–8 minutes. Carefully remove the pastry basket from the mould. This is an effective way to serve dressings.

The
SPRING
collection

Twenty delicious dishes without meat

Hot Crudite!

1 lb cauliflower florets 450 g	
Batter Mixture	
1 egg	
½ pint semi-skimmed milk 300 ml	
4 oz flour 100 g	
pinch salt	
Garlic Sauce	
½ pint semi-skimmed milk 300 ml	
1 onion clouté (see page 102)	
1 oz polyunsaturated margarine 25 g	
1 clove garlic, finely chopped	
1 oz flour 25 g	
salt and freshly ground pepper	
1–2 tsp chopped fresh parsley 5–10 ml	

Cook the cauliflower in boiling water, until just tender but still firm. Drain well and refresh.

To make the batter, gradually blend the egg and milk with the flour and salt until a smooth mixture is formed. Dip the cauliflower in the batter and deep-fry in hot fat until crisp and golden brown. Drain thoroughly.

To make the garlic sauce, heat the milk with the onion clouté. Melt the margarine in a pan, stir in the garlic and fry. Add the flour and make a roux. Remove the onion and add the milk gradually, stirring constantly to make a smooth sauce. Allow the sauce to cook. Season and add the chopped parsley.

Arrange in a serving dish with a small quantity of garlic sauce as a coulis. Serve the remaining sauce separately.

Variations

Use other vegetables, such as aubergines, courgettes or mushrooms, instead of the cauliflower.

Experiment with different sauces or dips, such as blue cheese sauce or yogurt and cucumber, instead of the garlic sauce.

Garnish spring onion fleuron; paprika; bread basket (see page 5); chicory leaf; lollorosso; endive; fresh thyme; sliced tomato; kiwi fruit

Protein – low
Fat – medium
Fibre – medium

Cashew Paella

1 tbsp   polyunsaturated oil   15 ml
1 medium onion, chopped
1 clove garlic, finely chopped
4 oz   brown rice   100 g
4 oz   long-grain rice   100 g
3 oz   cashew nuts   75 g
1 tsp   paprika   5 ml
1 tsp   chopped fresh basil   5 ml
1 tsp   turmeric   5 ml
1/2 red pepper, chopped
1/2 green pepper, chopped
2 sticks celery, chopped
15 oz   can tomatoes, chopped   425 g
3/4 pint   vegetable stock   450 ml
salt and freshly ground pepper

Heat the oil and fry the onion and garlic until soft. Add both types of rice, the cashew nuts, paprika, basil and turmeric, and cook for 2 minutes. Then add the peppers, celery, tomatoes and stock. Simmer until the rice is just cooked – about 30 minutes.

Press the mixture into individual pudding moulds, and turn out on to plates. Serve with tomato sauce (see page 96).

All brown rice can be used instead of an equal quantity of the long-grain variety, but this will give the dish a heavier texture, making it difficult to form the moulds.

Variations
Try different nuts instead of cashews, or a combination of varieties.

Add wild rice to the brown rice.

For a traditional but more expensive Paella, replace the paprika with saffron.

Garnish sliced baby sweetcorn (blanched); diced red and green pepper (blanched); sprigs of fresh thyme

Protein – low
Fat – medium
Fibre – medium

Delhi Lasagne

6 oz   lentils   175 g
3 oz   onion, chopped   75 g
1 clove garlic, finely chopped
2 tsp   garam masala   10 ml
1 tbsp   polyunsaturated oil   15 ml
1/2 pint   vegetable stock   300 ml
1 tsp   coriander   5 ml
salt and freshly ground pepper
8 oz   lasagne verdi   225 g
3 oz   low-fat Cheddar cheese, grated   75 g
toasted cooked lentils
Sauce
1 oz   polyunsaturated margarine   25 g
1 oz   flour   25 g
1/2 pint   semi-skimmed milk   300 ml
salt and freshly ground pepper

Soak the lentils as required (see page 4). Drain.

Sauté the onion, garlic and garam masala in the oil. Add the lentils and stir so that they are covered with the onion mixture. Mix in the stock. Bring to the boil and simmer gently, uncovered, for about 45 minutes, until the lentils are tender and the mixture thick. Stir in the coriander and season with pepper.

Cook the lasagne in boiling, salted water until tender, then drain thoroughly. Meanwhile make the sauce. Melt the margarine, add the flour and make a roux. Add the milk gradually and heat, stirring constantly, to make a smooth sauce. Allow to cook before stirring in half the cheese.

In an ovenproof dish, layer the pasta, lentil mixture and sauce, finishing with a layer of the sauce. Sprinkle the top with the remaining grated cheese and toasted lentils. Bake at 400°F/200°C/gas mark 6 for 45–50 minutes, until golden brown.

Garnish slices of radish; baby sweetcorn; spring onion fleuron

Protein – high
Fat – medium
Fibre – high

Lentil Roast

8 oz   lentils   225 g
4 oz   low-fat Cheddar cheese, grated   100 g
1 onion, finely chopped
1 tsp   chopped fresh parsley   5 ml
pinch cayenne pepper
1 tbsp   lemon juice   15 ml
salt and freshly ground pepper
1 medium egg
chopped nuts

Soak the lentils as required (see page 4). Drain, put into a pan and cover with fresh cold water. Bring to the boil and boil rapidly for 10 minutes. Reduce the heat and simmer for 20–30 minutes. Check after 10 minutes, in case more water is needed. The mixture should cook to a stiff purée. Mix in the grated cheese, chopped onion, parsley, cayenne pepper and lemon juice. Season to taste.

Beat the egg lightly and mix into the lentil mixture. If the mixture is too moist, add some wholemeal breadcrumbs. Press the mixture into an oiled 1-lb/450-g loaf tin. Sprinkle lightly with chopped nuts. Bake at 375°F/190°C/gas mark 5 for 45–50 minutes, until the top is golden brown and the mixture feels firm to the touch.

Leave to stand for 10 minutes in the tin before turning out. Serve with a sauce, such as mushroom (see page 96).

Variations
Divide the lentil mixture into three parts and layer with 8 oz/225 g sliced tomatoes.

Use yellow split peas instead of lentils.

Garnish oyster mushrooms; sliced carrot; spring onion rings; sliced blackberry; fresh chervil

Protein – high
Fat – low
Fibre – medium

Soufflé Pancakes

Pancakes

4 oz	wholemeal flour	100 g
	pinch salt	
	1 egg, beaten	
½ pint	semi-skimmed milk	300 ml
	polyunsaturated oil	

Soufflé Filling

1 oz	polyunsaturated margarine	25 g
1 oz	flour	25 g
¼ pint	semi-skimmed milk	150 ml
	4 eggs	
	salt and freshly ground pepper	
2 oz	low-fat Cheddar cheese, grated	50 g
2 oz	walnuts, finely chopped	50 g

To make the pancakes, sieve the flour and salt. Add the beaten egg and milk and blend to make a smooth batter. Make eight 6-in/15-cm pancakes.

To prepare the soufflé filling, melt the margarine, add the flour and cook for 3 minutes without allowing to colour. Blend in the milk gradually, stirring over a low heat until the sauce thickens and allow to cook. Leave the mixture to cool slightly and then add 2 whole eggs and 1 egg yolk (use remaining egg yolk in another recipe). Beat well and add seasoning and half the grated cheese. Turn the mixture into a bowl and stir in the walnuts. Whisk the remaining egg whites with a pinch of salt until stiff, add half to the soufflé mixture and mix well. Fold in the remaining egg white carefully.

Put about 2 tbsp/30 ml of the soufflé filling across the centre of each pancake and roll up carefully. Arrange in a well-oiled dish and sprinkle with the remaining cheese. Bake at 400°F/200°C/gas mark 6 for 15–20 minutes. Serve immediately.

Garnish yogurt and cream sauce; pinch of chopped fresh parsley; pinch of paprika; fresh thyme

Protein – high
Fat – high
Fibre – medium

Harvest Crumble

Crumble Topping

2 oz	polyunsaturated margarine	50 g
4 oz	wholemeal flour	100 g
1 oz	rolled oats	25 g
2 oz	low-fat Cheddar cheese, grated	50 g
1 oz	walnuts, chopped	25 g

Filling

1 oz	polyunsaturated margarine	25 g
5 oz	celery, diced	150 g
4 oz	red onions, chopped	100 g
6 oz	white cabbage, sliced	175 g
6 oz	baby turnips, diced	175 g
2 oz	baby sweetcorn, sliced	50 g
1 oz	wholemeal flour	25 g
¼ pint	vegetable stock	150 ml
6 oz	canned tomatoes, chopped	175 g
¼ pint	semi-skimmed milk	150 ml
2 tsp	chopped fresh parsley	10 ml
	salt and freshly ground pepper	

To make the crumble topping, rub the margarine into the flour and oats, then stir in the cheese and walnuts.

To make the filling, melt the margarine in a pan and sweat the celery, onion, cabbage, turnip and sweetcorn for 2 minutes. Sprinkle with the flour, stir and cook for a further 2 minutes. Gradually add the stock. Add the tomatoes, milk, parsley, salt and pepper, and bring to the boil, stirring constantly, until the sauce thickens. Allow to cook.

Put the filling into a dish and cover with the crumble topping. Bake at 375°F/190°C/gas mark 5 for 20 minutes, or until the crumble has browned.

Variation
Add crumbled blue cheese instead of Cheddar and replace the margarine with nut butter in the topping.

Garnish chopped fresh parsley; green pepper filled with tomato, celery head, turnip, red onion and baby sweetcorn

> Protein – medium
> Fat – high
> Fibre – high

Gumbo Stew

5 oz   dried haricot beans   150 g
8 oz   okra   225 g
2 tbsp   polyunsaturated oil   30 ml
1 onion, chopped
1 clove garlic, finely chopped
1 green pepper, chopped
1 green chilli, sliced
15 oz   canned tomatoes, chopped   425 g
2 oz   tomato purée   50 g
salt and freshly ground pepper
2 tsp   chopped fresh mixed herbs (thyme, chives, basil and oregano)   10 ml
1 tsp   raw cane sugar   5 ml
1 tsp   red wine vinegar   5 ml
1 pint   vegetable stock, made with 1 stock cube   600 ml
salt and freshly ground pepper

Soak the haricot beans overnight (see page 4). Drain, rinse and put in a pan of cold water. Bring to the boil and cook rapidly for 10 minutes. Reduce the heat and simmer for about 1½ hours. Drain. Alternatively use 1 lb/450 g canned or cooked haricot beans.

To prepare the okra, wash and dry, then cut off the stems without damaging or breaking open the pods.

Heat the oil in a pan and stir-fry the okra, onion and garlic for 5 minutes. Add the pepper, chilli, tomatoes, tomato purée, seasoning and herbs. Stir in the stock. Bring to the boil and simmer for 15 minutes. Stir in the sugar and vinegar. Simmer for a further 5 minutes and serve.

Suggested Presentation
Using a small flan ring, make a base with the haricot beans. Top with the gumbo, remove the flan ring and garnish.

Garnish red onion rings; spring onion fleuron; radish; chicory; fresh oregano

Protein – medium
Fat – medium
Fibre – high

Canneloni Verdi

12 canneloni verdi tubes or lasagne verdi sheets
2 tbsp polyunsaturated oil 30 ml
3 oz onions, chopped 75 g
1 clove garlic, finely chopped
6 oz mushrooms, sliced 175 g
12 oz courgettes, sliced 350 g
1 tsp fresh oregano, chopped 5 ml
6 oz canned tomatoes, chopped 175 g
1 tbsp tomato purée 15 ml
salt and freshly ground pepper
1 oz Parmesan cheese 25 g
Sauce
1 oz polyunsaturated margarine 25 g
1 oz flour 25 g
½ pint semi-skimmed milk 300 ml
1 onion clouté (see page 102)
2 oz Ricotta cheese 50 g

If using lasagane sheets, cook in boiling water until tender. Drain and refresh.

Heat the oil and sauté the onion and garlic. Add the mushrooms and courgettes and sauté. Add the oregano, tomatoes, tomato purée and sauté for 2–3 minutes. Add a little vegetable stock or water. Cover and cook gently for 10–15 minutes, then season to taste.

To make the sauce, heat the milk with the onion clouté. Melt the margarine in a pan, add the flour and make a roux. Remove the onion and add the milk gradually. Heat, stirring constantly, until the sauce thickens. Allow to cook. Add the Ricotta cheese.

Spoon a little of the vegetable mixture into the canneloni tubes. Alternatively, spoon the mixture on to the lasagne sheets and roll up.

Arrange in a dish and cover generously with the sauce. Sprinkle with the Parmesan and bake at 350°F/180°C/gas mark 4 for 30 minutes.

Variation
Replace the vegetables with a sauce made from cooked beans and tomatoes.

Garnish canelled and sliced courgette; fresh basil

Protein – high
Fat – high
Fibre – high

Harvest Pancakes

4 oz   plain wholemeal flour   100 g
pinch salt
pinch ground nutmeg
1 egg, beaten
½ pint   semi-skimmed milk   300 ml
polyunsaturated oil

To make the batter, sieve the flour, salt and nutmeg. Add the beaten egg and milk and blend to make a smooth batter. Make eight 6-in/15-cm pancakes. Fill the pancakes with the chosen filling and serve immediately.

Suggested Fillings

Ratatouille and grated cheese (allow 2 oz/50 g cheese per serving)

Creamed spinach and Parmesan cheese, as shown in the photograph garnished with paprika and mint leaves (top the pancakes with Béchamel and yogurt cheese sauce, see page 96)

Cooked lentils and cashew nuts mixed with natural yogurt

Asparagus, mushrooms, leeks or broccoli in a soured cream or Béchamel sauce

Sweetcorn and red or green pepper in a mustard sauce (allow ½ pint/300 ml Béchamel sauce, see page 96, flavoured with wholegrain mustard for 4 servings)

Fromage frais with herbs (allow 3 oz/75 g low-fat fromage frais per serving)

Stir-fried vegetables (fry some spring onions, peas, beansprouts, mushrooms and walnuts; add a soy sauce thickened with a little cornflour)

Variations

Use different flours and add such ingredients as chopped spinach, herbs and nuts to the batter mixture.

Fold the pancakes into envelopes; roll into cornets; stack to make a cake, layered with filling, and cut into wedges to serve.

Garnish natural yogurt; fresh mint; pinch of paprika

Analysis for Pancake only:

Protein – low
Fat – medium
Fibre – low

Baked Broccoli with Tomato

1 lb fresh broccoli 450 g	
2 oz polyunsaturated margarine 50 g	
3 oz onions, finely chopped 75 g	
1 clove garlic, finely chopped	
4 oz mushrooms, sliced 100 g	
2 oz wholemeal flour 50 g	
2 tbsp tomato purée 30 ml	
¾ pint vegetable stock 450 ml	
4 oz canned tomatoes, chopped 100 g	
2 oz low-fat Cheddar cheese, grated 50 g	
2 oz Mozzarella cheese, diced 50 g	
salt and freshly ground pepper	

Cook the broccoli lightly until just tender. Drain and place in an ovenproof dish.

Melt the margarine and cook the onion, without colouring. Add the garlic and mushrooms and cook for 2 minutes. Stir in the flour and cook for 5 minutes, stirring constantly. Add the tomato purée. Stir in the stock and bring to the boil. Add the tomatoes, salt and pepper. Bring back to the boil and adjust the seasoning.

Pour the tomato sauce evenly over the broccoli. Mix the Cheddar and Mozzarella together and sprinkle on top. Bake at 350°F/180°C/gas mark 4 for 30 minutes. Serve with rosti or hash brown potatoes.

Variation
Top with a nutty charlotte or crumble mixture.

Garnish spring onion and cucumber shavings; mustard and cress

Protein – medium
Fat – medium
Fibre – medium

Singapore Stroganoff

1 tbsp	polyunsaturated oil 15 ml
3 oz	onions, sliced 75 g
4 oz	mixed peppers, cut in strips 100 g
4 oz	carrots, cut in thin strips 100 g
4 oz	courgettes, cut in thin strips 100 g
3 oz	water chestnuts, sliced 75 g
1 tsp	fresh thyme, chopped 5 ml
2 oz	mixed chopped nuts, toasted 50 g
8 oz	wholewheat spaghetti 225 g
	chopped fresh parsley

Sauce

1 oz	polyunsaturated margarine 25 g
4 oz	mushrooms, sliced 100 g
1 oz	flour 25 g
½ pint	semi-skimmed milk 300 ml
3 oz	low-fat soft cheese 75 g
	pinch ground nutmeg
2 fl oz	natural yogurt 60 ml
	salt and freshly ground pepper

To make the sauce, melt the margarine and sauté the mushrooms. Add the flour to make a roux. Gradually add the milk and heat, stirring, to make a smooth sauce. Allow to cook. Stir in the soft cheese and season well. Just before serving, stir in the yogurt.

Reserve some vegetables for garnish and blanch in boiling water for 30 seconds.

Heat the oil and sauté the onion. Add the peppers, carrots, courgettes, water chestnuts and thyme and sauté without allowing to colour. Season with salt and pepper. Put the mixture in an earthenware dish. Cover with the sauce, arrange blanched vegetables and top with the mixed nuts.

Serve with wholewheat spaghetti or noodles, or brown rice.

Garnish spring onion fleuron; radicchio; fresh chervil; curly endive; sliced mushrooms

Protein – medium
Fat – medium
Fibre – high

Italian-style Peppers

4 large whole peppers (red, yellow or green)
Filling
4 oz   mushrooms, sliced   100 g
6 oz   brown rice, cooked   175 g
2 tsp   chopped fresh parsley   10 ml
1 tsp   chopped mixed fresh herbs (thyme, basil, chives and oregano)   5 ml
2 oz   fresh or frozen peas   50 g
4 oz   mixed nuts, coarsely chopped   100 g
1 oz   polyunsaturated margarine   25 g
1 oz   wholemeal flour   25 g
8 fl oz   semi-skimmed milk   240 ml
2 fl oz   natural yogurt   60 ml
2 oz   Mozzarella cheese, sliced   50 g
salt and freshly ground pepper

Prepare the peppers (see page 5).

To make the filling, cook the mushrooms gently in their own juices. Stir in the rice, parsley, mixed herbs, peas and nuts. Season well. Melt the margarine in another pan, add the flour and make a roux. Add the milk gradually, stirring over a low heat until the sauce thickens. Allow to cook, then add the yogurt, taking care that the sauce does not boil. Bind the rice mixture with the sauce and fill the peppers. Top with the Mozzarella slices. Replace the lids.

Arrange the peppers in a greased ovenproof dish. Bake at 400°F/200°C/gas mark 6 for about 40 minutes, until tender. Cover with greased paper for the first 20 minutes. Serve with a coulis of Béchamel sauce (see page 96) and lace with tomato sauce (see page 96) (using a fork to twirl sauces lightly) as shown in the photograph.

Variation
Replace the rice with cooked bulgur wheat (see page 102).

Garnish chicory; lollorosso; snipped fresh chives

| Protein – medium |
| Fat – high |
| Fibre – medium |

Chickpeas Provençale

3 oz   dried chickpeas   75 g
2 tbsp   polyunsaturated oil   30 ml
8 oz   onions, diced   225 g
2   large aubergines, cut into cubes
4 oz   yellow peppers, cut into strips   100 g
4 oz   red peppers, cut into strips   100 g
8 oz   courgettes, sliced   200 g
1 clove garlic, finely chopped
15 oz   canned tomatoes, chopped   425 g
2 tbsp   tomato purée   30 ml
½ pint   vegetable stock   300 ml
1 fresh bay leaf
2 tsp   chopped mixed fresh herbs (thyme, basil, chives and oregano)   10 ml
1 lb   fresh noodles, mixed spinach and egg   450 g
or
8 oz   dried noodles   225 g
salt and freshly ground pepper

Soak the chickpeas overnight (see page 4). Drain, rinse and put in a pan of cold water. Bring to the boil and cook rapidly for 10 minutes. Reduce the heat and simmer for 1–1½ hours. Drain. Alternatively use 8 oz/225 g canned or cooked chickpeas.

Heat the oil and sauté the onion until tender. Add the aubergine, peppers, courgette and garlic and continue to cook, covered, until the vegetables are soft. Stir in the tomatoes, tomato purée, stock and chickpeas. Add the bay leaf and mixed herbs. Season with salt and pepper and simmer, uncovered, for 20–30 minutes.

Serve with noodles.

Variations
Stuff green peppers with the mixture and bake until the peppers are tender.

Replace the noodles with brown rice.

Garnish thin slices of fennel; fresh oregano; fresh thyme

Protein – high
Fat – medium
Fibre – high

Vegetable Cheesecake

Base
3 oz   polyunsaturated margarine   75 g
3 oz   wholemeal breadcrumbs, toasted   75 g
2 oz   oatmeal   50 g
pinch ground nutmeg
Topping
3 oz   onions, finely chopped   75 g
1 clove garlic, finely chopped
1 tbsp   polyunsaturated oil   15 ml
3 oz   courgettes, finely sliced   75 g
3 oz   carrots, finely sliced   75 g
1 tsp   fresh basil or rosemary, finely chopped   5 ml
1 tsp   finely chopped fresh parsley   5 ml
8 oz   cottage cheese and curd cheese, mixed   225 g
1 oz   Parmesan cheese   25 g
2 eggs
salt and freshly ground pepper

Melt the margarine and add the breadcrumbs, oatmeal, nutmeg and seasoning. Press the breadcrumb mixture into the base of an oiled flan dish.

Sauté the onion and garlic in the oil until softened. Add the vegetables and herbs and cook gently until tender. Season with salt and pepper. Meanwhile, beat together the cheeses and eggs. Combine with the vegetables. Turn the mixture into the flan dish and bake at 375°F/190°C/gas mark 5 for about 20 minutes, until set. Serve hot or cold.

Variations
Vary the vegetable content or try different herbs.

Serve a spicy tomato sauce (see page 97) as an accompaniment.

Use tofu (beancurd) instead of the cottage and curd cheeses.

Garnish cherry tomato flower; fresh basil leaves; pink grapefruit slices; raspberries

Protein – high
Fat – high
Fibre – medium

Suppli

1 oz   polyunsaturated margarine   25 g
4 oz   onion, chopped   100 g
12 oz   long-grain rice   350 g
2 fl oz   dry white wine   60 ml
1¾ pint   vegetable stock   1 litre
½ tsp   saffron   2.5 ml
3 eggs
1 oz   Parmesan cheese, grated   25 g
2 tbsp   semi-skimmed milk   30 ml
4 oz   Mozzarella cheese, cut in ½-in/1-cm cubes   100 g
1 oz   flour   25 g
2 oz   wholemeal breadcrumbs   50 g
polyunsaturated oil for frying
salt and freshly ground pepper

Melt the margarine and sauté the onion until tender. Add the rice and stir until the grains are coated. Add the wine, half the stock, saffron, salt and pepper. Bring back to the boil, stirring well, and simmer until the liquid has evaporated. Add the remaining stock. Reduce the heat and cook, uncovered, until the liquid has been absorbed. Leave to cool.

Beat 2 of the eggs lightly with the Parmesan cheese and combine with the rice mixture. Beat the remaining egg with the milk for the egg wash. Mould the rice mixture into small cakes or balls. Put a cube of cheese in the centre of each. Dip first in the flour, then the egg wash and coat with the breadcrumbs.

Fry in hot oil until golden brown. Drain and serve with a spicy sauce (see page 98).

Variation
Add different fresh herbs to the rice mixture, such as parsley, dill, thyme or tarragon.

Garnish feathered cherry tomato; curly endive; fresh rosemary; chopped spring onion tops; chopped nuts

Protein – high
Fat – medium
Fibre – medium

Lentil and Cauliflower Spice

8 oz	lentils 225 g
2 tbsp	polyunsaturated oil 30 ml
4 oz	onion, finely chopped 100 g
1 tsp	ground turmeric 5 ml
	few drops chilli sauce
1 tsp	ground cumin 5 ml
1 tsp	ground coriander 5 ml
	½ lime
	1 cauliflower
¾ pint	vegetable stock 450 ml
1 oz	shredded coconut 25 g
2 tsp	potato flour (fecule) 10 ml
2 tbsp	cold water 30 ml
2 oz	cashew nuts 50 g
	salt and freshly ground pepper

Soak the lentils as required (see page 4). Drain, rinse and put in a pan of cold water. Bring to the boil and cook rapidly for 10 minutes. Drain.

Heat the oil and fry the onion. As it softens, add the spices. Stir well and cook for 30 seconds. Add the lentils and stir well to ensure each grain is coated. Squeeze in the lime juice. Break the cauliflower into florets and add, with the vegetable stock and coconut. Bring to the boil and simmer for 20 minutes. If a thicker sauce is required, mix the potato flour with the cold water to form a paste and stir in. Add the cashew nuts and simmer until the cauliflower is just cooked. Correct the seasoning with salt and pepper.

Serve on a bed of saffron rice or with naan bread. Wedges of lime would make a refreshing accompaniment.

Garnish sliced spring onion tops; pinch of paprika; shredded coconut; toasted cashews; feathered cherry tomato; sprig of fresh oregano

Protein – high
Fat – high
Fibre – high

Lentil Duchesse

8 oz	lentils 225 g
2 oz	polyunsaturated margarine 50 g
1 onion, chopped	
1 clove garlic, finely chopped	
1 stick celery, chopped	
4 oz	carrots, grated 100 g
4 oz	mushrooms, sliced 100 g
½ tsp	fresh thyme, chopped 2.5 ml
½ tsp	fresh marjoram, chopped 2.5 ml
1 tsp	tomato purée 5 ml
vegetable stock	
1½ lb	potato, creamed 675 g
salt and freshly ground pepper	

Soak the lentils as required (see page 4). Drain, rinse and put in a pan of cold water. Bring to the boil and cook rapidly for 10 minutes. Reduce the heat and simmer for 20–30 minutes. Drain.

Melt the margarine and sweat the vegetables for about 10 minutes until tender. Then add the lentils, herbs, tomato purée and salt and pepper, mixing thoroughly. Add a little vegetable stock if the mixture appears dry.

Spoon the lentil mixture into an oiled, shallow, ovenproof dish or individual dishes. Spread or pipe the creamed potato on top and bake at 400°F/200°C/gas mark 6 for 30–40 minutes, until golden-brown.

Variations
Serve with a tomato or mushroom sauce (see page 96).

Add chopped nuts to the potato to vary the texture.

Replace the lentils with cooked beans, such as aduki or black-eye.

Garnish sliced carrot; fresh thyme; chopped fresh parsley

Protein – high
Fat – medium
Fibre – high

Wild Green Risotto

1½ lb	broccoli 675 g
4 oz	onions, sliced 100 g
1 clove garlic, finely chopped	
½ oz	polyunsaturated margarine 10 g
2 tsp	chopped mixed fresh herbs (oregano, thyme, basil and chives) 10 ml
2 oz	polyunsaturated margarine 50 g
2 oz	wholemeal flour 50 g
2 tbsp	tomato purée 30 ml
1 pint	semi-skimmed milk 600 ml
4 oz	brown rice 100 g
1 oz	wild rice 25 g
1 tbsp	pine kernels 15 ml
pinch chopped fresh basil	
salt and freshly ground pepper	

Wash and cut the broccoli into florets. Reserve a few for garnish. Put the remainder in a large pan with a little water, the onion, garlic, ½ oz/10 g polyunsaturated margarine, herbs and seasoning. Bring to the boil, reduce the heat, cover and sweat the vegetables until tender but still crisp. Place in a greased, ovenproof dish.

Make the sauce by melting the margarine, adding the flour and cooking for 1–2 minutes over a low heat. Add the tomato purée and gradually add the milk. Heat, stirring constantly, until the sauce thickens. Season and allow to cook.

Cook both rices according to the instructions on the packets. Drain and mix with the pine kernels and basil. Combine with the sauce and pour over broccoli. Bake at 350°F/180°C/gas mark 4 for 15 minutes.

Variations
Use spring greens or purple sprouting broccoli instead of green broccoli.

Substitute sunflower seeds for the pine kernels, adding a little grated Parmesan cheese.

Mix toasted, flaked almonds with the rice.

Garnish cooked broccoli heads

Protein – *medium*
Fat – *medium*
Fibre – *high*

Wholesome Hotpot

5 oz	dried butter beans 150 g
6 oz	onions, chopped 175 g
6 oz	celery, chopped 175 g
6 oz	carrots, sliced 175 g
2 oz	leeks, sliced 50 g
½ pint	vegetable stock 300 ml
10 oz	potatoes, thinly sliced 275 g
1 oz	polyunsaturated margarine, melted 25 g
	salt and freshly ground pepper

Soak the butter beans overnight (see page 3). Drain, rinse and put in a pan of cold water. Bring to the boil and cook rapidly for 10 minutes. Reduce heat and simmer for about 1 hour. Drain. Alternatively use 1 lb/450 g canned or cooked butter beans.

Mix the beans with the onion, celery, carrot, leek, stock, salt and pepper. Spoon into individual serving dishes. Arrange the sliced potatoes on top and brush with the melted margarine. Bake at 350°F/180°C/gas mark 4 for 45–60 minutes.

Variations
To make a more substantial dish, add 1 oz/25 g wholegrain barley with the vegetables and stock.

Sprinkle with sesame seeds before putting in the oven to give a more unusual flavour.

Garnish spring onion fleuron and fresh dill; or endive, fresh dill, chopped fresh chives and sliced baby sweetcorn

Protein – low
Fat – low
Fibre – high

Aubergine and Courgette Bake

8 oz	aubergines, sliced 225 g
3 tbsp	polyunsaturated oil 45 ml
6 oz	courgettes, sliced 175 g
	flour for dusting
4 oz	onion, chopped 100 g
8 oz	canned tomatoes, chopped 225 g
	2 eggs
4 oz	curd cheese 100 g
¼ pint	natural yogurt 150 ml
1 oz	Parmesan cheese 25 g
	salt and freshly ground pepper

Sprinkle the aubergine slices with salt and allow to drain, Dry with absorbent kitchen paper.

Heat the oil. Dust the aubergines with flour and shallow-fry until golden and soft. Remove from the pan. Sauté the onion until soft. Add the tomatoes and simmer until the mixture reduces to a pulp. Leave to cool.

Beat the eggs with the curd cheese and yogurt. Combine with the cooled tomato mixture. Add seasoning. Put a layer of aubergines and courgettes in a greased ovenproof dish and cover with the tomato mixture. Sprinkle with the Parmesan cheese. Continue in layers, finishing with a topping of cheese. Bake at 375°F/190°C/gas mark 5 for 40 minutes, or until golden.

Variations
Use cottage cheese instead of curd cheese; for a more expensive alternative, try Ricotta cheese.

Replace the aubergines with sliced marrow.

Garnish tomato sauce (see page 96); segments of clementine; fresh chives; chopped fresh parsley

Protein – medium
Fat – high
Fibre – low

The
SUMMER
collection
Twenty delicious dishes without meat

'Hot' Peppers

6 oz	bulgur wheat 175 g
	4 peppers
2 tbsp	polyunsaturated oil 30 ml
4 oz	onions, chopped 100 g
2 tsp	chilli seasoning 10 ml
6 oz	canned tomatoes, chopped 175 g
2 tbsp	tomato purée 30 ml
1 tsp	ground cumin 5 ml
½ vegetable stock cube, crumbled
salt and freshly ground pepper
7 fl oz	natural yogurt 200 ml
3 oz	cucumber, finely chopped 75 g

Cover the bulgur wheat with twice its volume of cold water and soak for 20 minutes. Drain well. Meanwhile prepare the peppers (see page 5).

Heat the oil and sauté the onion with the chilli seasoning for 3–4 minutes. Add the tomatoes, tomato purée, cumin, crumbled stock cube, a little water and drained bulgur wheat. Cook, stirring, for 1–2 minutes. Add seasoning. Fill the peppers with the chilli mixture and replace the lids. Cover with greased foil and bake at 375°F/190°C/gas mark 5 for about 40 minutes.

Heat the yogurt gently with the cucumber. Whisk lightly, season and serve hot or cold as an accompaniment to the peppers.

Variation
Add finely diced vegetables such as mushrooms, courgettes or aubergines to the bulgur wheat.

Garnish lollorosso; celery top; fresh dill; snipped fresh chives; yogurt and cucumber dressing in a filo pastry basket (see page 5)

Protein – low
Fat – medium
Fibre – medium

Mushroom Crunch

	Crunch	
2 oz	polyunsaturated margarine	50 g
4 oz	fresh wholemeal breadcrumbs	100 g
3 oz	low-fat Cheddar cheese, grated	75 g
3 oz	mixed nuts, chopped	75 g
1 tsp	chopped fresh mixed herbs	5 ml
	1 clove garlic, finely chopped	
	Sauce	
2 oz	polyunsaturated margarine	50 g
4 oz	mushrooms, sliced	100 g
2 oz	flour	50 g
1 pint	semi-skimmed milk	600 ml
	salt and freshly ground pepper	
1 tsp	chopped fresh mixed herbs (oregano, chives, basil and chervil)	5 ml

To make the crunch, rub the margarine into the breadcrumbs, add the remaining ingredients and mix well. Shape into individual mounds and bake at 425°F/220°C/gas mark 7 for 15 minutes.

Meanwhile, melt the margarine for the sauce and sauté the mushrooms for a few minutes. Remove the mushrooms and reserve. Add the flour to the remaining liquid to make a roux, and gradually add the milk. Heat, stirring constantly, until the sauce thickens and allow to cook. Add the mushrooms, seasoning and mixed herbs. Spoon some of the sauce over each serving plate, place a crunch mound on each and coat with the remaining sauce.

Variation
Replace the mushrooms with other vegetables such as leeks, celery or asparagus.

Garnish yellow cherry tomato rose;
spring onion fleurons

Protein – high
Fat – high
Fibre – medium

Ratatouille

1 tbsp	polyunsaturated oil 15 ml
8 oz	onions, finely chopped 225 g
2 cloves garlic, finely chopped	
8 oz	courgettes, cut into 1 × ½-in/2.5 × 1-cm dice 225 g
8 oz	marrow, cut into 1 × ½-in/2.5 × 1-cm dice 225 g
1 lb	fresh tomatoes, skinned and chopped, or canned tomatoes, chopped 450 g
2 red peppers, roughly chopped	
1 tsp	chopped fresh parsley 5 ml
1 vegetable stock cube, crumbled	
1 tsp	chopped fresh basil 5 ml
salt and freshly ground pepper	

Heat the oil and sweat the onion and garlic until soft. Add all the remaining ingredients, cover and simmer for 30 minutes.

Serve with wholewheat pasta, brown rice or potatoes or as a side dish to accompany a flan or savoury bake.

Variations
Use as a base for other dishes, such as ratatouille crumble or as a filling for savoury pancakes.

Add cooked chickpeas or lentils to increase the protein content.

Garnish blanched, finely diced green and red peppers; chopped fresh parsley

Protein – low
Fat – low
Fibre – low

Croquettes Mont Blanc

1 lb	parsnips, swede, or a variety of root vegetables, diced 450 g
½ pint	semi-skimmed milk 300 ml
2 oz	onion, finely chopped 50 g
1 oz	polyunsaturated margarine 25 g
1 tsp	chopped fresh chives 5 ml
	1 egg, beaten
2 oz	chestnuts, finely chopped 50 g
2 oz	wholemeal flour 50 g
	salt and freshly ground pepper

Coating

	1 egg
2 tbsp	semi-skimmed milk 30 ml
4 oz	fresh breadcrumbs 100 g
	polyunsaturated oil for frying

Sauce

1 oz	polyunsaturated margarine 25 g
1 oz	flour 25 g
½ pint	semi-skimmed milk 300 ml
3 oz	low-fat soft cheese 75 g

Put the parsnips in a pan with the milk, bring to the boil and simmer, uncovered, until tender and most of the liquid has been absorbed. Drain off any excess liquid, then mash. Sauté the onion until soft. Add the margarine, onion, chives, egg, chestnuts and flour to the parsnip mixture. Season well and chill until firm.

To make the sauce, melt the margarine, add the flour and cook gently for 1–2 minutes. Gradually add the milk and heat, stirring constantly, until the sauce thickens. Allow to cook before stirring in the cheese.

Lightly whisk the egg and milk for the coating. Just before serving, shape the parsnip mixture into balls. Dip each into the egg wash and roll in breadcrumbs. Deep- or shallow-fry the croquettes for about 5 minutes, until golden-brown. Serve hot or cold, topped with the cheese sauce and accompanied by a crisp salad.

Variation

A red wine or cranberry sauce would make a suitable alternative to the cheese sauce.

Garnish grated Parmesan cheese; paprika; celery tops

Protein – high
Fat – medium
Fibre – high

Lima Bean Curry

6 oz	dried butter beans	175 g
1 tbsp	polyunsaturated oil	15 ml
4 oz	onions, chopped	100 g
1 clove garlic, finely chopped		
1 tsp	curry powder	5 ml
1 tsp	paprika	5 ml
8 oz	canned tomatoes, roughly chopped	225 g
1 lb	potatoes, peeled and cubed	450 g
2 fresh bay leaves		
¾ pint	vegetable stock	450 ml
4 oz	peas, fresh or frozen	100 g
salt and freshly ground pepper		

Soak the butter beans overnight (see page 3). Drain, rinse and put in a pan of cold water. Bring to the boil and cook rapidly for 10 minutes. Reduce heat and simmer for 1–1½ hours. Drain. Alternatively use 1 lb/450 g canned or cooked beans.

Heat the oil and sauté the onion and garlic for 5 minutes; do not allow to turn brown. Stir in the spices and cook for a few minutes before adding the tomatoes. Cover and simmer for a further 5 minutes, then add the potatoes and bay leaves. Add the stock and stir well. Simmer gently until the potatoes are nearly cooked, add the butter beans, peas and seasoning and cook for a further 5–6 minutes.

Serve accompanied by mixed brown and white rice, combined with beansprouts (one part to four parts rice), pressed into a dariole mould and turned out on to a tomato sauce base.

Variation
Add 2 oz/50 g raisins or sultanas and 1 tbsp/15 ml apricot jam to give the curry a slightly sweet taste.

Garnish sliced kiwi fruit; chopped fresh parsley; thinly sliced black olive; sprig of fresh dill

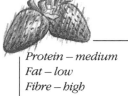

Protein – medium
Fat – low
Fibre – high

Capsicum and Chickpea Couscous

3 oz	dried chickpeas 75 g
8 oz	couscous 225 g
2 tbsp	polyunsaturated oil 30 ml
4 oz	onions, chopped 100 g
1 aubergine. diced	
1 red pepper, diced	
1 green pepper, diced	
2 carrots, sliced	
½ tsp	ground cumin 2.5 ml
½ tsp	ground coriander 2.5 ml
½ tsp	turmeric 2.5 ml
8 oz	canned tomatoes, chopped 225 g
1 tbsp	tomato purée 15 ml
½ pint	vegetable stock 300 ml
2 courgettes, sliced	
2 oz	sultanas or raisins 50 g
2 tsp	chopped fresh parsley 10 ml
salt and freshly ground pepper	

Soak the chickpeas overnight (see page 4). Drain, rinse, put in a pan of cold water. Bring to the boil and cook rapidly for 10 minutes. Reduce heat and simmer for 1–1½ hours. Drain. Alternatively use 8 oz/225 g canned or cooked chickpeas.

Soak the couscous in cold water for 15 minutes, drain. Heat the oil, add the onion, aubergine, peppers and carrot and sauté for 5 minutes, stirring frequently. Stir in the cumin, coriander, turmeric, tomatoes, tomato purée and stock. Bring to the boil and stir well. Cover and simmer for 20 minutes. Add the chickpeas, courgettes, sultanas and seasoning. Stir well. Cover and simmer for a further 20 minutes. Cook couscous according to instructions on the packet.

Spread the couscous over a serving dish and fluff up with a fork. Add the parsley to the vegetable mixture and serve with the couscous.

Variation
Other grains, such as bulgur or cracked wheat, can be substituted for the couscous.

Garnish diced peppers, blanched; fresh thyme; fresh basil (on couscous)

Protein – low
Fat – medium
Fibre – medium

Marrow Almondine

1 medium marrow, thickly sliced
2 onions, chopped
2 tbsp   polyunsaturated oil   30 ml
1 red pepper, chopped
4 oz   mushrooms, sliced   100 g
4 oz   ground almonds   100 g
4 oz   wholemeal breadcrumbs   100 g
2 eggs, beaten together with ¼ pint/150 ml water
1 tsp   chopped fresh mixed herbs (oregano, chives, basil and chervil)   5 ml
1 oz   skimmed milk powder   25 g
salt and freshly ground pepper
2 tbsp   tomato purée   30 ml
2 tomatoes, sliced
4 oz   Mozzarella cheese   100 g
1 oz almonds 25 g

Remove the seeds from the marrow. Boil the marrow slices for 5 minutes and refresh.

Sauté the onions in the oil. Add the red pepper and mushrooms and sauté for 1–2 minutes. Mix with the ground almonds, breadcrumbs, eggs, herbs, skimmed milk powder and seasoning to obtain a moist mixture. Spread the marrow slices with tomato purée and pile on the filling. Top with sliced tomatoes, Mozzarella cheese and a sprinkling of almonds. Bake at 350°F/180°C/gas mark 4 for 30 minutes and serve with barbecue sauce (see page 98).

Variation
Replace the eggs with almond butter.

Garnish toasted almonds; sliced baby sweetcorn; finely chopped green pepper

Protein – high
Fat – high
Fibre – high

Garbanzo Fritters

7 oz   dried chickpeas   200 g
1 small onion, quartered
2 cloves garlic, finely chopped
4 oz   wholemeal bread   100 g
½ tsp   cumin seeds   2.5 ml
3 small red chillies, crushed
1 egg, beaten
2 tsp   chopped fresh parsley   10 ml
salt and freshly ground pepper
2 oz   wholemeal breadcrumbs   50 g
vegetable oil for deep-frying
4 wholemeal pitta breads, warmed
endive, onion and tomato slices

Soak chickpeas overnight (see page 4). Drain, rinse, put in a pan of cold water, bring to the boil and cook rapidly for 10 minutes. Reduce heat and simmer for 1–1½ hours. Drain. Alternatively use 1 lb 5 oz/600 g canned or cooked chickpeas.

Place chickpeas, onion, garlic, bread, cumin seeds and chillies in a food processor. Process until smooth and turn into a bowl. Add egg, parsley and seasoning and mix well. Form the mixture into eight balls. Coat each ball in breadcrumbs and flatten to give an oval shape.

Half-fill a deep-fryer or deep saucepan with oil. Heat to 375°F/190°C and fry the chickpea fritters for about 3 minutes. Drain well. Cut each pitta bread in half, cut a fritter in half and place inside the pitta with a little endive, a few slices of onion and tomato. Serve hot, with barbecue sauce (see page 98).

Variation
Serve with a refreshing relish, a lemon-flavoured mayonnaise or a yogurt dressing.

Garnish lollorosso; Chinese leaves; radicchio; fresh thyme

Protein – high
Fat – low
Fibre – high

Nutty Burgers

4 oz	onions, chopped 100 g
1 tbsp	polyunsaturated oil 15 ml
4 oz	mixed nuts, finely chopped 100 g
4 oz	peanuts, finely chopped 100 g
1 oz	peanut butter 25 g
5 oz	wholemeal breadcrumbs 150 g
1 tsp	chopped fresh mixed herbs (thyme, basil, oregano and chives) 5 ml
1 tsp	chopped fresh parsley 5 ml
	salt and freshly ground pepper

Sauté the onion in the oil, then stir in the mixed nuts, peanuts, peanut butter, breadcrumbs, herbs and seasoning. Mix well, add sufficient stock to bind. Shape the mixture into burgers. Put on oiled tray and bake at 400°F/200°C/gas mark 6 for 30 minutes, turning once.

Serve with a tomato or corn relish, or a hot tomato sauce.

Variation
Add other vegetables or different nuts to enhance this basic nut burger recipe.

Garnish half tomato sauce (see page 96), half cheese sauce (see page 96) on serving plate; 1 burger topped with tomato and fresh oregano; 1 burger topped with melted Mozzarella; celery top

Protein – medium
Fat – high
Fibre – medium

Omelette Collection

Omelette (serves 1)

3 eggs
salt and freshly ground pepper
cold water
½ oz   polyunsaturated margarine   10g

Whisk the eggs with seasoning and a dash of water. Melt the margarine in an omelette pan. When it begins to foam, pour in the egg and as it sets, break up lightly with a fork, ensuring all the mixture is cooked. Add the chosen filling and when the base is lightly browned, fold and tip on to a serving dish.

Suggestions for Fillings

Spinach omelette: chopped spinach, mixed with small cubes of Mozzarella cheese (as shown in the photograph), served with a tomato sauce (see page 96), garnished with feathered cherry tomato, parsley, red chicory, Chinese leaf, rosemary and thyme.

Nutty mushroom omelette: sliced mushrooms, sautéd with mixed chopped nuts and a little yeast extract.

Pasta omelette: mix cooked wholewheat pasta into the egg mixture prior to cooking. Pour into the pan and cook as for the basic omelette. Sprinkle Parmesan cheese in the centre before turning out.

Spanish omelette: sauté chopped onions with diced green and red peppers. Add the egg mixture and cook without breaking up. When just set, turn the omelette over until the base is lightly browned. Do not fold.

Analysis for Omelette only:

Protein – low
Fat – medium
Fibre – low

Cheddar Roast

1 oz	polyunsaturated margarine 25 g
3 oz	onions, chopped 75 g
4 oz	carrots, grated 100 g
4 oz	mixed nuts, chopped 100 g
4 oz	wholemeal bread 100 g
½ pint	vegetable stock 300 ml
1 tsp	yeast extract 5 ml
2 tsp	chopped fresh mixed herbs (oregano, chives, thyme and basil) 10 ml
	few drops Worcestershire sauce
	salt and freshly ground pepper
	2 tomatoes, sliced
2 oz	low-fat Cheddar cheese, grated 50 g

Melt the margarine and sauté the onions; add the carrots and continue to sauté. Remove from the heat. Grind the nuts and bread together. Heat the vegetable stock with the yeast extract together until just boiling. Combine all the ingredients except the tomatoes and cheese and gradually add sufficient stock to obtain a firm mixture. Half-fill four small pudding moulds or a loaf tin with the mixture and cover with a layer of sliced tomato and grated cheese, then fill with the remaining mixture. Bake at 350°F/180°C/gas mark 4 for 30 minutes, or until golden-brown.

Turn out and serve with a mushroom sauce (see page 96).

Variation
Omit the cheese and tomato to give a basic nut roast which can be served hot or cold or used as a filling for sandwiches and jacket potatoes.

Garnish sliced mushrooms; sliced baby sweetcorn; feathered cherry tomato; celery top; lollorosso; fresh rosemary and thyme

Protein – medium
Fat – high
Fibre – medium

Gardener's Delight

8 oz	wholemeal shortcrust pastry	225 g
1 oz	polyunsaturated margarine	25 g
1 oz	flour	25 g
½ pint	semi-skimmed milk	300 ml
4 oz	low-fat Cheddar cheese, grated	100 g
	salt and freshly ground pepper	
3 oz	carrots, grated	75 g
3 oz	leeks, thinly sliced	75 g
3 oz	peas, fresh or frozen	75 g
3 oz	sweetcorn kernels	75 g

Line one large or four individual flan rings with the pastry and bake blind (see page 102).

To prepare the sauce, melt the margarine, add the flour and cook gently for 1–2 minutes. Gradually stir in the milk and heat, stirring constantly, until the sauce thickens. Allow to cook before adding half the cheese. Season. Combine the cheese sauce with all the vegetables. Divide the mixture evenly between the flans. Sprinkle with the remaining grated cheese and bake at 375°F/190°C/gas mark 5 for 30 minutes.

Variations
Use different flours, buckwheat for example, to make a more unusual pastry.

Vary the texture by adding nuts or oatmeal to the pastry.

Garnish sliced cherry tomato; sliced spring onion; redcurrants; fresh flat-leaf parsley

Protein – high
Fat – high
Fibre – high

Summer Vegetables with Wild Rice

3 oz	white rice 75 g
3 oz	brown rice 75 g
2 oz	wild rice 50 g
1 cauliflower, broken into florets	
8 oz	courgettes, diced 225 g
4 oz	green beans, cut in 1-in/2.5-cm lengths 100 g
4 oz	peas, fresh or frozen 100 g
1 tbsp	lemon juice 15 ml
1 oz	polyunsaturated margarine 25 g
salt and freshly ground pepper	

Sauce

1 oz	polyunsaturated margarine 25 g
1 oz	flour 25 g
½ pint	semi-skimmed milk 300 ml
2 oz	Parmesan cheese, grated 50 g
2 tsp	chopped fresh parsley 10 ml
2 tsp	pesto sauce 10 ml
1 tsp	sesame seeds, toasted 5 ml

Prepare and cook each type of rice according to the instructions on the packet. Meanwhile, steam the vegetables until just tender. Remove from the heat and toss with the lemon juice, margarine and seasoning.

To make the sauce, melt the margarine, stir in the flour and cook gently for 1–2 minutes. Gradually add the milk and heat, stirring constantly, until the sauce thickens. Allow to cook, then add half the Parmesan cheese, all the parsley and pesto sauce.

To serve, drain the white, brown and wild rice and mix them together. Arrange in a serving dish. Pile the vegetables on top. Cover with the sauce and sprinkle with the remaining Parmesan mixed with sesame seeds. Lightly brown under the grill.

Variations

Replace the rice with a wholewheat pasta.

Substitute other vegetables in season.

Garnish cherry tomatoes; celery top; fresh chervil

Protein – medium
Fat – medium
Fibre – medium

'Crisp' Savoury Cheesecake

Base		
1 oz	plain unsalted potato crisps	25 g
4 oz	wholewheat bran biscuits	100 g
1 oz	mixed nuts, chopped	25 g
3 oz	polyunsaturated margarine	75 g

Topping		
4 oz	blue cheese, softened	100 g
4 oz	low-fat cream cheese, softened	100 g
1 tsp	mustard	5 ml
1 tsp	snipped fresh chives	5 ml
	salt and freshly ground pepper	
7 fl oz	double cream, lightly whipped	200 ml

To prepare the base, crush the crisps and biscuits until they resemble fine crumbs. Mix in the nuts. Melt the margarine, add the crumbs and mix well. Press the mixture into one large or four individual flan dishes. Chill.

Beat the cheeses together. Add the mustard, chives and seasoning and mix. Stir in the cream, blending well. Turn out on to the base, level with a knife and chill until set.

Serve topped with spinach purée on a tomato coulis.

Garnish spring onion shavings;
cranberries; finely ground nuts

Protein – medium
Fat – high
Fibre – medium

Haricot and Potato Pie

4 oz   dried haricot beans   100 g
4 oz   onion, chopped   100 g
1 clove garlic, finely chopped
1 tbsp   polyunsaturated oil   15 ml
1 lb   courgettes, sliced   450 g
7 fl oz   vegetable stock   200 ml
5 oz   canned tomatoes, chopped   150 g
2 tbsp   tomato purée   30 ml
2 tbsp   semi-skimmed milk   30 ml
1 oz   spring onion, finely chopped   25 g
1 lb   creamed potatoes   450 g
salt and freshly ground pepper

Soak the haricot beans overnight (see page 4). Drain, rinse and put in a pan of cold water. Bring to the boil and cook rapidly for 10 minutes. Reduce the heat and simmer for about 1 hour. Drain. Alternatively use 12 oz/350 g canned or cooked haricot beans.

Sweat the onion and garlic in the oil. Add the courgettes, stock, tomatoes, tomato purée and seasoning and bring to the boil. Simmer for 10 minutes. Add the beans and put in a serving dish.

Beat the milk, spring onion, salt and pepper into the creamed potatoes. Spread or pipe the mixture over the vegetables and bake at 350°F/180°C/gas mark 4 for 30–40 minutes.

Variation
Use different types of bean and vary the base vegetable.

Garnish sliced courgette; fresh mint leaves

Protein – low
Fat – low
Fibre – high

Sweet 'n' Sour Rissoles

8 oz	brown rice	225 g
1 oz	polyunsaturated margarine	25 g
4 oz	onions, chopped	100 g
1 oz	wholemeal breadcrumbs	25 g
4 oz	walnuts, finely ground	100 g
½ tsp	chopped fresh thyme	2.5 ml
½ tsp	chopped fresh sage	2.5 ml
4 oz	canned tomatoes, chopped	100 g
1 tsp	soy sauce	5 ml
	1 egg, beaten	
	polyunsaturated oil for frying	
Sauce		
4 oz	canned apples	100 g
	pinch ground cinnamon	

Cook the rice and refresh well. Melt the margarine and sauté the onion until soft. Mix with the rice, breadcrumbs, walnuts and herbs. Combine with the tomatoes and soy sauce and sufficient egg to bind, adding more breadcrumbs if the texture is too moist. Shape the mixture into rissoles. Shallow-fry in polyunsaturated oil for 3 minutes on each side.

To make the sauce, purée the apples, add the cinnamon and heat gently.

Serve the rissoles hot with green vegetables or a salad, accompanied by the apple sauce.

Garnish sauce of natural yogurt and pesto; puréed apple flavoured with honey; feathered apples; tomato rose; celery tops; radish slices; walnut halves

Protein – low
Fat – high
Fibre – medium

Aubergine Parcels

4 oz   lentils   100 g
8 oz   aubergine, diced   225 g
1   onion, chopped
4 tbsp   polyunsaturated oil   60 ml
1   red pepper, seeded and diced
1 tsp   ground cumin   5 ml
1 tsp   ground cinnamon   5 ml
1 tsp   curry paste   5 ml
salt and freshly ground pepper
4 oz   Caerphilly cheese, diced   100 g
2 tsp   chopped fresh oregano   10 ml
8 oz   filo pastry   225 g
1   egg
2 tbsp   semi-skimmed milk   30 ml

Soak the lentils as required (see page 4). Drain, rinse and put in a pan of cold water. Bring to the boil and cook rapidly for 10 minutes. Reduce the heat and simmer for 20–30 minutes. Drain and cool.

Sprinkle the aubergine with salt and leave to drain in a colander for 30 minutes. Rinse thoroughly and dry, using absorbent kitchen paper. Sauté the onion in half the oil until soft. Add the aubergine and red pepper and cook for 2–3 minutes. Stir in the spices and curry paste and continue to cook for a further 2 minutes. Season and leave to cool. Stir in the lentils, cheese and oregano.

To make the parcels: place one layer of filo pastry on a work surface. Brush with water. Lay a second layer on top and brush with water. Cut into four 6-in/15-cm squares. Brush all the edges of the pastry with water. Pile a portion of the aubergine mixture in the centre of each square. Bring up the corners and sides of the pastry to form a parcel shape. Beat the egg with the milk and egg wash the parcels. Place on a greased baking tray and cook at 325°F/170°C/gas mark 3 for 30 minutes, or until the pastry is golden-brown. Serve hot or cold.

Variation
Substitute artichoke hearts for the aubergine.

Garnish spring onion fleuron; fresh thyme

Protein – medium
Fat – high
Fibre – medium

Pasta del Bria

6 oz	pasta shapes (egg, spinach and tomato) 175 g
1 lb	cauliflower, broken into florets 450 g
8 oz	leeks, sliced 225 g
4 oz	flat or button mushrooms, sliced 100 g
2 oz	polyunsaturated margarine 50 g
2 oz	flour 50 g
1 pint	semi-skimmed milk 600 ml
	salt and freshly ground pepper
6 oz	low-fat Cheddar cheese, grated 175 g

Cook the pasta in boiling, salted water until just tender. Drain, refresh and set aside.

Cook the cauliflower and leeks in boiling, salted water until just tender. Drain well, put in an ovenproof dish and keep warm. Cook the mushrooms in their own juices, drain and add to the cauliflower and leeks.

To prepare the sauce, melt the margarine, stir in the flour and cook for 1–2 minutes. Gradually add the milk and seasoning and bring to the boil, stirring constantly. Allow the sauce to cook. Stir in the pasta and half of the cheese. Slowly bring the mixture back to boiling point.

Pour the sauce over the vegetables, sprinkle with the cheese and place under the grill until golden-brown.

Variation
Mix sesame seeds with grated cheese to provide a more unusual topping.

Garnish leek shavings; sliced radish; chicory leaves; sliced spring onion; black olives

Protein – high
Fat – medium
Fibre – high

Courgette Crunch

1 tbsp   polyunsaturated oil   15 ml
4 oz   onions, chopped   100 g
1 clove garlic, finely chopped
1 lb   courgettes, canelled and thinly sliced   450 g
salt and freshly ground pepper
15 oz   canned tomatoes, chopped   425 g
2 tbsp   tomato purée   30 ml
1 oz   polyunsaturated margarine   25 g
½ pint   semi-skimmed milk   300 ml
1 oz   flour   25 g
2 oz   wholemeal breadcrumbs, toasted   50 g
3 oz   low-fat Cheddar cheese, grated   75 g
2 tsp   chopped fresh mixed herbs (oregano, thyme, chives and basil)   10 ml
1 oz   mixed nuts, chopped   25 g

Heat the oil and sauté the onions and garlic until soft. Add the courgettes, seasoning and oregano and cook for 5 minutes. Add the tomatoes, tomato purée, and a little water or vegetable stock if required. Simmer for about 10 minutes, until the courgettes are just cooked.

To prepare the sauce, melt the margarine, add the flour and cook gently for 1–2 minutes. Gradually add the milk and heat, stirring constantly, until the sauce thickens. Allow to cook.

Transfer the vegetables to a serving dish. Cover with the sauce. Mix the breadcrumbs, cheese, herbs and nuts together and sprinkle over the top. Place under the grill until brown and bubbling.

Garnish sliced courgettes; fresh flat-leaf parsley

Protein – medium
Fat – high
Fibre – low

Aubergine Layer

1½ lb	aubergines, cut into ½-in/1-cm slices 675 g
4 oz	courgettes, sliced 100 g
4 tbsp	polyunsaturated oil 60 ml
4 oz	onions, finely diced 100 g
4 oz	sweet peppers, diced 100 g
	1 clove garlic, finely chopped
	1 tsp fennel seeds 5 ml
½ tsp	chopped fresh oregano 2.5 ml
15 oz	canned tomatoes, chopped 425 g
	salt and freshly ground pepper
8 oz	Mozzarella cheese, finely sliced 225 g
4 oz	wholemeal breadcrumbs 100 g
2 oz	Parmesan cheese, grated 50 g

Sprinkle the aubergine slices with salt and leave to drain. Dry slices and brush both sides with a little oil. Place on a baking tray and bake at 400°F/200°C/gas mark 6 for 30–45 minutes, until lightly browned and tender. Blanch and refresh the courgettes.

Meanwhile, make a thick tomato sauce. Heat the oil and sauté the onions, but do not allow to turn brown. Add the peppers, garlic, fennel seeds, oregano, tomatoes, a little water and seasoning. Bring to the boil and simmer for 30 minutes.

In an ovenproof dish, place a layer of aubergines and courgettes, top with a layer of tomato sauce and Mozzarella. Repeat layers, finishing with the Mozzarella. Combine the breadcrumbs and Parmesan cheese and sprinkle thickly over the top. Bake at 375°F/190°C/gas mark 5 for 30 minutes.

Garnish endive; fresh flat-leaf parsley; mange-tout; cranberries

Protein – medium
Fat – high
Fibre – high

The
AUTUMN
collection
Twenty delicious dishes without meat

Sweet 'n' Sour Vegetables

6 oz potatoes, cut into 1 × ½-in/2.5 × 1-cm batons 175g	
3 oz carrots, canelled and sliced 75 g	
3 oz courgettes, canelled and sliced 75 g	
2 oz dessert apple, diced 50 g	
4 oz red pepper, cut into 1 × ½-in/2.5 × 1-cm batons 100 g	
½ pint vegetable stock 300 ml	
3 oz mushrooms, sliced 75 g	
3 oz canned tomatoes, chopped 75 g	
2 oz water chestnuts, sliced 50 g	
Sauce	
1 tbsp polyunsaturated oil 15 ml	
4 oz onions, chopped 100 g	
1 clove garlic, finely chopped	
1 tbsp tomato purée 15 ml	
1 tbsp soy sauce 15 ml	
2 tbsp white wine vinegar 30 ml	
1 tbsp dry sherry (optional) 15 ml	
1 tsp ground ginger 5 ml	
1 oz soft brown sugar 25 g	
1 tbsp chopped mixed nuts 15 ml	
salt and freshly ground pepper	
½ oz arrowroot 10 g	

Reserve some vegetables to blanch for garnish. Cook the potatoes, carrots, courgettes, apple and red pepper in a little of the stock for 10 minutes, until just tender. In a separate pan, soften the mushrooms and tomatoes in a little more stock. Add to the other vegetables with the water chestnuts.

In a large pan or wok, heat the oil and gently cook the onion and garlic.

Combine the remaining sauce ingredients except the arrowroot with the remaining stock and add to the onion and garlic, stirring well. Blend the arrowroot with a little water and add to the sauce.

Add the vegetables to the sauce, stir and bring to the boil. Reduce the heat and simmer for 5 minutes. Serve with a mixture of long-grain white rice and wild rice.

Variation
Serve with noodles or as a filling for baked potatoes.

Garnish blanched vegetables; chopped fresh parsley

Protein – low	
Fat – low	
Fibre – low	

Lentil Moussaka

4 oz	lentils 100 g
4 tbsp	polyunsaturated oil 60 ml
4 oz	onions, chopped 100 g
1 clove garlic, finely chopped	
4 oz	mushrooms, sliced 100 g
¼ pint	vegetable stock 150 ml
2 tbsp	tomato purée 30 ml
1 tsp	chopped fresh oregano 5 ml
½ tsp	ground nutmeg 2·5 ml
12 oz	aubergines, sliced, salted and drained 350 g
2 tomatoes, skinned and sliced	
2 potatoes, boiled and sliced	
salt and freshly ground pepper	

Sauce

1 oz	polyunsaturated margarine 25 g
1 oz	flour 25 g
½ pint	semi-skimmed milk 300 ml
2 oz	low-fat Cheddar cheese, grated 50 g
pinch dry mustard	
salt and freshly ground pepper	

Soak the lentils as required (see page 4). Drain, rinse and put in a pan of cold water. Bring to the boil and cook rapidly for 10 minutes. Reduce the heat and simmer for 20–30 minutes.

Heat 2 tbsp/30 ml of the oil and sauté the onions and garlic gently. Add the mushrooms and lentils and cook for a few more minutes. Mix in the stock, tomato purée and oregano. Season well and add the nutmeg and remove from the heat. Sauté the aubergine slices in the remaining oil until soft.

Spread the lentil mixture over the base of an oiled ovenproof dish, cover with the aubergine slices, then a layer of tomato slices and top with the potato slices.

To make the sauce, melt the margarine, add the flour and cook gently for 1–2 minutes. Gradually add the milk and stir over a gentle heat until the sauce thickens. Allow to cook before adding 1 oz/25 g of the cheese and the mustard. Season. Pour the sauce over the moussaka and sprinkle with the remaining cheese. Bake at 350°F/ 180°C/gas mark 4 for 20 minutes, or until the cheese is golden-brown and bubbling.

Variation
Replace the lentils with cooked mixed beans.

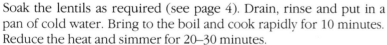

Garnish fresh rosemary; tomato; chopped spring onion tops

Protein – medium
Fat – high
Fibre – high

Sweet 'n' Savoury Loaf

4 oz	peanuts, finely chopped	100 g
5 oz	carrots, grated	150 g
5 oz	celery, finely chopped	150 g
2 oz	dessert apple, grated	50 g
3 oz	wholemeal breadcrumbs	75 g
1 tsp	chopped fresh mixed herbs (thyme, basil, oregano and sage)	5 ml
	salt and freshly ground pepper	
	1 egg	
4 tbsp	semi-skimmed milk	60 ml
2 tsp	tomato purée	10 ml

Mix the peanuts, carrots, celery, apple, breadcrumbs, herbs and seasoning. Combine with the egg, milk and tomato purée, and mix thoroughly. If the mixture is too moist, add more breadcrumbs. Press the mixture into a greased 1-lb/450-g loaf tin or individual pudding moulds and bake at 350°F/180°C/gas mark 4 for 30–35 minutes.

Turn out and serve with a spinach sauce (see page 96).

Variations
To make a more substantial dish, combine the ingredients with cooked brown rice. Cook as above but serve from the tin.

Serve with a tomato sauce.

Garnish carrot slices; baby sweetcorn slices; celery tops

Protein – low
Fat – medium
Fibre – medium

Macaroni Crisp

1 oz	polyunsaturated margarine 25 g
4 oz	onions, chopped 100 g
1 clove garlic, finely chopped	
15 oz	canned tomatoes, chopped 425 g
1 tsp	chopped fresh oregano 5 ml
salt and freshly ground pepper	
1 lb	fresh broccoli 450 g
4 oz	wholewheat or egg macaroni 100 g
7 fl oz	natural yogurt 200 ml
2 oz	Roquefort cheese 50 g
1 oz	Mozzarella cheese 25 g
1 oz	rolled oats 25 g

Melt the margarine and sauté the onions and garlic. Add the tomatoes, oregano, ½ pint/300 ml cold water and seasoning and simmer for about 20 minutes. Cook the broccoli in boiling, salted water until just tender; drain and refresh. In a separate pan, cook the macaroni in boiling water for 10–15 minutes, until just tender; drain and refresh.

In an ovenproof dish, layer half the tomato sauce and macaroni. Add the broccoli. Repeat the layers of sauce and macaroni.

Beat the yogurt and cheeses together, spread over the macaroni and sprinkle evenly with the oats. Bake at 400°F/200°C/gas mark 6 for 30 minutes, or until the top is lightly browned.

Serve with a light mint-flavoured Béchamel (see page 96).

Variations
Replace the broccoli with another vegetable, such as cauliflower or courgettes.

Use wholewheat pasta shapes instead of the macaroni.

Garnish sliced tomato; endive; fan of cucumber slices; radish flower; fresh thyme

Protein – medium
Fat – medium
Fibre – medium

Butter Bean Kiev

8 oz	dried butter beans 225 g
5 oz	wholemeal breadcrumbs 150 g
	salt and freshly ground pepper
1 oz	polyunsaturated margarine 25 g
	1 onion, diced
	1 egg
2 tbsp	semi-skimmed milk 30 ml
	polyunsaturated oil for frying

Garlic Butter

3 oz	butter 75 g
	2 cloves garlic, finely chopped
1 tsp	chopped fresh parsley 5 ml

Soak the butter beans overnight (see page 3). Drain, rinse, and put in a pan of cold water. Bring to the boil and cook rapidly for 10 minutes. Reduce the heat and simmer for about 1½ hours. Drain. Alternatively use 1½ lb/675 g canned or cooked butter beans.

To prepare the garlic butter, soften the butter and blend in the garlic and parsley. Roll in greaseproof paper and chill until firm.

Mash the butter beans and mix in 3 oz/75 g of the breadcrumbs and seasoning. Melt the margarine and sauté the onion until soft, but do not allow to turn brown. Add the onion to the butter bean mixture and mix well. Shape the mixture into four cutlets. Place a cube or slice of garlic butter in the centre of each cutlet, and mould the mixture around it.

Lightly whip the egg with the milk and seasoning. Egg wash each cutlet and coat with the remaining breadcrumbs. Sauté each side of the cutlets until golden-brown. Alternatively, grill or bake the cutlets, turning once. Serve with a selection of chutneys.

Variations
Use any other cooked bean as the base of the cutlets.

Replace the garlic butter with a herb- or lemon-flavoured butter, or slices of cheese.

Garnish feathered tomato; cucumber; fresh chervil; sliced blackcurrant

Protein – medium	
Fat – high	
Fibre – high	

Mexican Chickpeas

6 oz	dried chickpeas 175 g
1 tbsp	polyunsaturated oil 15 ml
4 oz	onions, finely chopped 100 g
½ tsp	chilli powder 2.5 ml
1 tsp	ground cumin 5 ml
2 red or green peppers, finely chopped	
2 tbsp	tomato purée 30 ml
12 fl oz	vegetable stock 360 ml
lemon juice	
salt and freshly ground pepper	

Soak the chickpeas overnight (see page 4). Drain, rinse, put in a pan of cold water. Bring to the boil and cook rapidly for 10 minutes. Reduce the heat and simmer for 1–1½ hours. 'Alternatively use 1 lb/450 g canned or cooked chickpeas.

Heat the oil in a large pan and fry the onions and spices gently for 5 minutes. Add the peppers and chickpeas and stir. Dissolve the tomato purée in the stock and add to the vegetables. Stir well and cook for 10 minutes. Add seasoning and a little lemon juice.

Serve with a mixture of white, brown and wild rice combined with finely diced red or green peppers.

Variation
Serve with wholewheat pasta or toasted pitta bread and a crisp salad.

Garnish tortilla chips; spring onions; celery top; lollorosso

Protein – low
Fat – medium
Fibre – high

Vegetable Stir-fry

1 tbsp	polyunsaturated oil 15 ml
3 oz	onions, sliced 75 g
1 clove garlic, finely chopped	
3 oz	carrot, cut into batons 75 g
½ green pepper, cut into batons	
4 oz	broccoli, broken into small florets 100 g
4 oz	baby sweetcorn 100 g
6 oz	tomatoes, chopped 175 g
3 tbsp	cider vinegar 45 ml
1 oz	soft brown sugar 25 g
½ pint	pineapple juice 300 ml
1 vegetable stock cube, crumbled	
2 tsp	soy sauce 10 ml
1 tsp	ground ginger 5 ml
salt and freshly ground pepper	
4 oz	bamboo shoots 100 g
2 oz	water chestnuts, sliced 50 g
1 tbsp	arrowroot 15 ml

Heat the oil in a large pan or wok. Add the onion, garlic and carrots and sauté until the onion is soft. Add the pepper, broccoli, sweetcorn and tomatoes. Combine the vinegar, sugar, pineapple juice, crumbled stock cube and soy sauce and pour over the vegetables. Add the ginger, a little water and seasoning and stir well. Bring to the boil, reduce the heat, cover and simmer, skimming occasionally until the vegetables are tender but still crisp.

Stir in the bamboo shoots and water chestnuts. Blend the arrowroot with a little water, add to the stir-fry, mix well and cook for a further 2 minutes. Serve immediately.

Variations
Serve the stir-fry with brown rice or wholewheat noodles.

Use the stir-fry as a filling for pancakes, or as a layer in a nut roast.

Garnish chopped fresh parsley

Protein – low
Fat – low
Fibre – low

Chickpeas Wellington

5 oz	dried chickpeas 150 g
2 tsp	yeast extract 10 ml
5 oz	Brazil nuts, ground 150 g
5 oz	wholemeal breadcrumbs 150 g
4 oz	onions, finely chopped 100 g
6 oz	mushrooms, sliced 175 g
	vegetable stock
2 tsp	fresh mixed herbs, chopped 10 ml
	salt and freshly ground pepper
8 oz	flaky pastry 225 g
	1 egg
2 tbsp	semi-skimmed milk 30 ml

Soak the chickpeas overnight (see page 4). Drain, rinse and put in a pan of cold water. Bring to the boil and cook rapidly for 10 minutes. Reduce the heat and simmer for about 1½ hours. Drain. Alternatively use 1 lb/450 g canned or cooked chickpeas.

Put the chickpeas with the yeast extract, Brazil nuts and breadcrumbs into a food processor and blend. Sauté the onions and mushrooms until they produce their own liquid, then add the chickpea mixture to the pan, adding sufficient vegetable stock to obtain a firm mixture. Add the herbs and seasonings and mix thoroughly.

Mould the mixture into a loaf shape. Roll out the flaky pastry and use to wrap the loaf, covering it completely. Beat the egg and milk together and egg wash the pastry. Bake at 400°F/200°C/gas mark 6 for 20–30 minutes, or until the pastry is crisp and lightly browned.

Serve with tomato sauce (see page 96).

Variations
Replace the Brazils with other types of nut.

Serve with an apple or cranberry sauce.

Garnish tomato coulis; fresh rosemary

Protein – high
Fat – high
Fibre – high

Kebab with Nut Risotto

For each Kebab
2 slices red onion
2 chunks red pepper
5 slices courgette
3 button mushrooms
2 chunks green pepper
2 cherry tomatoes
1 oz   polyunsaturated margarine, melted   25 g
Risotto (serves 4)
2 oz   polyunsaturated margarine   50 g
8 oz   long-grain brown rice   225 g
1 pint   boiling water   600 ml
4 oz   mushrooms, thinly sliced   100 g
2 oz   peas, cooked   50 g
2 oz   roasted peanuts, halved   50 g
or
2 oz   walnuts, roughly chopped   50 g
2 oz   Parmesan cheese, grated   50 g
1 tbsp   lemon juice. 15 ml
salt and freshly ground pepper

On to a kebab stick or long skewer, thread a slice of onion, a chunk of red pepper, a slice of courgette, a mushroom, a chunk of green pepper and a tomato; repeat. Brush the vegetables with margarine and grill, turning frequently, for about 10 minutes.

To make the risotto, melt the margarine and fry the rice gently for a few minutes. Pour on the boiling water and cook the rice for about 25–30 minutes, or until tender; most of the water should have been absorbed. Stir in the sliced mushrooms, peas, nuts and grated cheese and heat through for 5 minutes. Add the lemon juice and seasoning.

Serve the kebabs and risotto with barbecue sauce (see page 98).

Variation
Consider other combinations for the kebabs, such as tofu, eggs, artichoke hearts and aubergines.

Garnish red chicory; Chinese leaves; fresh rosemary; fresh flat-leaf parsley

Protein – medium
Fat – high
Fibre – medium

Garden Pizza

Base	
½ oz dried yeast 10 g	
3 tbsp warm water 45 ml	
6 oz wholemeal flour 175 g	
pinch baking powder	
1 oz polyunsaturated margarine 25 g	
3 tbsp semi-skimmed milk 45 ml	
Topping	
3 oz onions, finely diced 75 g	
1 clove garlic, finely chopped	
1 tbsp polyunsaturated oil 15 ml	
6 tbsp tomato purée 85ml	
8 oz canned tomatoes, chopped 225 g	
pinch fresh chopped basil	
pinch fresh chopped oregano	
3 oz sweet peppers, diced 75 g	
3 oz mushrooms, sliced 75 g	
2 oz canned artichokes, sliced (optional) 50 g	
5 oz Mozzarella cheese, diced 150 g	

Dissolve the yeast in the warm water and set aside until it froths. Meanwhile, sift the flour and baking powder. Cut the margarine into small cubes, add to the flour and gently fold in. Stir in the milk and yeast mixture and mix to a stiff dough. Knead lightly and leave to prove for 30 minutes. Roll out the dough to ½-in/1-cm thick and slightly raise the edges.

To make the topping: sauté the onions and garlic in the oil. Add the tomato purée, chopped tomatoes and herbs and simmer for 15 minutes. Season generously. Meanwhile, lightly sauté the peppers and mushrooms.

Spread the tomato sauce on the base. Arrange the vegetables and top with sliced artichokes. Sprinkle with the cheese. Bake the pizza at 450°F/230°C/gas mark 8 for 15–18 minutes.

Variations

Experiment with different toppings and try making individual pizzas.

Use a different flour or add ingredients such as oats, herbs, garlic or chopped spinach to the dough, or, for speed, use a pizza base mix.

Garnish red pepper: lollorosso; Chinese leaves; celery top; fresh basil; fresh rosemary; red chilli

Protein – high
Fat – medium
Fibre – medium

Chilli Sin Carne

5 oz	dried kidney beans 150g
1 tbsp	polyunsaturated oil 15 ml
6 oz	onions, chopped 150 g
	1 red pepper, diced
	1 green pepper, diced
	1 stick celery, diced
15 oz	canned tomatoes, chopped 425 g
2 tbsp	tomato purée 30 ml
½ tsp	chilli powder 2·5 ml
	pinch cayenne
½ tsp	ground cumin 2·5 ml
1 tsp	chopped fresh oregano 5 ml
	salt and freshly ground pepper
½ pint	vegetable stock 300 ml

Soak the kidney beans overnight (see page 4). Drain, rinse and put in a pan of cold water. Bring to the boil and cook rapidly for 10 minutes. Reduce the heat and simmer for about 1 hour. Drain. Alternatively use 1 lb/450 g canned or cooked kidney beans.

Heat the oil and sauté the onion, peppers and celery until tender. Add the beans, tomatoes, tomato purée, chilli powder, cayenne, cumin and oregano. Season well. Add the stock and simmer for about 30 minutes, until the flavours blend and the chilli thickens slightly.

Serve with a mixture of white, brown and wild rice.

Variations
Stuff green peppers with chilli sin carne and bake until peppers are tender.

Use as a jacket potato topping.

Serve topped with soured cream or guacamole.

Use as a filling for a pasty.

Garnish snipped fresh chives; sliced pitta bread; endive; fresh mint

Protein – medium
Fat – low
Fibre – high

Mushroom Envelopes

1 tbsp	polyunsaturated oil 15 ml
6 oz	onions, finely chopped 175 g
1 clove garlic, finely chopped
8 oz	mushrooms, sliced 225 g
1 tsp	chopped fresh mixed herbs (basil, chives, oregano and thyme) 5 ml
pinch cayenne
3 eggs, hard-boiled
salt and freshly ground pepper
8 oz	puff pastry 225 g
1 egg
2 tbsp	semi-skimmed milk 30 ml

Heat the oil and sauté the onion and garlic for 3–4 minutes, then add the mushrooms, herbs and cayenne. Cover and sweat until tender. Remove from the heat and cool.

Separate the hard-boiled eggs. Mash the yolks, chop the whites and add both to the mushroom mixture. Season.

Roll out the pastry and cut into four 6-in/15-cm circles. Beat the egg and milk together and use to brush the edges of the pastry. Spoon 1–2 tablespoons of the filling into the centre of each pastry circle, fold the pastry over and seal the edges. Egg wash, pierce a hole in the top and bake at 425°F/220°C/gas mark 7 for 15–20 minutes.

Serve with mushroom sauce (see page 96).

Variation
Use a wholemeal pastry but this will give a heavier texture to the envelopes.

Garnish radicchio; celery tops; sliced mushrooms; chopped fresh parsley

Protein – low
Fat – high
Fibre – low

Sag Madras

3 oz	dried chickpeas 75 g
1 oz	polyunsaturated margarine 25 g
4 oz	onions, chopped 100 g
1 clove garlic, finely chopped	
1 tsp	turmeric 5 ml
1 tsp	ground coriander 5 ml
½ tsp	ground ginger 2.5 ml
1 tsp	garam masala 5 ml
½ tsp	mixed spice 2.5 ml
1 tbsp	mild curry powder 15 ml
6 oz	potatoes, cubed 175 g
½ pint	vegetable stock 300 ml
1 tbsp	tomato purée 15 ml
6 oz	fresh leaf spinach 175 g
6 oz	canned tomatoes, chopped 175 g
6 oz	mushrooms, sliced 175 g
salt and freshly ground pepper	

Soak chickpeas overnight (see page 4). Drain, rinse and put in a pan of cold water. Bring to the boil and cook rapidly for 10 minutes. Reduce the heat and simmer for about 1½ hours. Drain. Alternatively use 8 oz/225 g canned or cooked chickpeas.

Melt the margarine and sauté the onions and garlic. Add all the spices and cook for 2 minutes. Add the potatoes, chickpeas, stock and tomato purée and simmer for 15 minutes. Add the remaining ingredients and simmer for a further 10 minutes.

Serve with brown rice and naan bread. Yogurt would make a refreshing accompaniment.

Garnish radish rose; fresh parsley; spring onion fleuron; chopped spring onion

Protein – low
Fat – medium
Fibre – medium

Swiss Potato Croquettes

1 lb potatoes 450 g	
2 oz polyunsaturated margarine 50 g	
2 eggs	
pinch ground nutmeg	
salt and freshly ground pepper	
3 oz wholemeal breadcrumbs 75 g	
2 tsp chopped fresh mixed herbs (oregano, basil, chives and thyme) 10 ml	
1 oz Parmesan cheese, grated 25 g	
4 oz Gruyère cheese, diced 100 g	
2 tbsp flour 30 ml	

Boil and mash the potatoes. Add the margarine and 1 egg, the nutmeg and seasonings and mix well. Allow to cool. Meanwhile, mix the breadcrumbs, herbs and Parmesan cheese. Beat the remaining egg.

Shape the potato mixture into croquettes, putting some diced Gruyère in the centre of each one. Dip the croquettes first in the seasoned flour, then the beaten egg and finally the breadcrumb mixture. Bake on an oiled baking tray at 350°F/180°C/gas mark 4 for about 30 minutes, until golden-brown, turning once. Alternatively, deep-fry the croquettes for 2–3 minutes.

Serve with a spicy sauce, such as hot barbecue (see page 98), laced with natural yogurt, or chilled yogurt flavoured with mint.

Garnish celery tops; fresh chervil

Protein – medium
Fat – high
Fibre – medium

Harvest Burger

5 oz	dried mixed beans (eg: kidney, black-eye and haricot) 150 g
1 tbsp	polyunsaturated oil 15 ml
4 oz	onions, finely chopped 100 g
1 clove garlic, finely chopped	
¼ pint	vegetable stock 150 ml
2 tbsp	tomato purée 30 ml
1 tsp	chopped fresh mixed herbs (oregano, thyme, chives and basil) 5 ml
1 tsp	paprika 5 ml
salt and freshly ground pepper	
1 oz	wholemeal flour 25 g
2 oz	Mozzarella cheese, melted 50 g
2 tomatoes, sliced	
4 burger buns	

Soak the beans overnight (see page 3). Drain, rinse and put in separate pans of cold water. Bring to the boil and cook rapidly for 10 minutes. Reduce the heat and simmer for the required time. Drain. Alternatively use 1 lb/450 g canned or cooked beans.

Heat the oil and sauté the onion and garlic until soft. Add the stock and bring to the boil. Add the beans, tomato purée, herbs, paprika and seasonings. Simmer the mixture until the liquid has evaporated.

Allow the mixture to cool, then mash and mould into burgers. Coat lightly in flour and chill. Grill the burgers on both sides for about 3 minutes and serve, topped with melted Mozzarella and sliced tomato inside a burger bun.

Variation
Coat the burgers with wholemeal breadcrumbs, then fry and serve with a tomato or barbecue sauce (see pages 96 and 98).

Garnish chicory; lollorosso; mustard and cress; spring onion fleurons; celery top; endive

Protein – medium
Fat – low
Fibre – high

Spinach and Blue Cheese Lasagne

8 oz	wholewheat lasagne	225 g
1 oz	Parmesan cheese, grated	25 g

Mushroom Layers

2 tsp	polyunsaturated oil	10 ml
6 oz	mushrooms, sliced	175 g
1 oz	wholemeal flour	25 g
½ pint	vegetable stock	300 ml
1 tsp	yeast extract	5 ml

Spinach and Cheese Layers

12 oz	fresh spinach	350 g
2 oz	polyunsaturated margarine	50 g
2 oz	flour	50 g
1 pint	semi-skimmed milk	600 ml
	salt and freshly ground pepper	
	pinch ground nutmeg	
2 oz	blue cheese, crumbled	50 g

Cook the lasagne in boiling water until tender; drain and refresh. Meanwhile, heat the oil and sweat the mushrooms until cooked. Boil the spinach until just cooked; drain off excess water, refresh and chop roughly.

To prepare the sauce for the mushroom layers, mix the flour to a smooth paste with a little of the stock in a pan. Stir in the remaining stock, together with the yeast extract. Bring to the boil and simmer for 2–3 minutes; add the mushrooms. Cook for 1–2 minutes, then remove from the heat.

To prepare the sauce for the spinach and cheese layers, melt the margarine, add the flour and cook gently for 1–2 minutes. Add the milk gradually and stir the sauce over the heat until thickened. Allow the sauce to cook, then remove from the heat and stir in seasoning and nutmeg. Mix half the sauce with the spinach and blue cheese.

In an ovenproof dish, layer the pasta, mushroom sauce, and spinach and cheese sauce, finishing with a layer of pasta. Pour the remaining sauce over the top and sprinkle with Parmesan cheese. Bake at 400°F/200°C/gas mark 6 for 30 minutes, or until bubbling.

Garnish spinach purée; sliced mushrooms; turned mushroom; paprika

Protein – high
Fat – medium
Fibre – high

Egg Bombay

1½ lb   broccoli   675 g
5 eggs, hard-boiled
2 tbsp   mango chutney, chopped   30 ml
salt and freshly ground pepper
2 oz   polyunsaturated margarine   50 g
6 oz   onions, finely chopped   175 g
1 tbsp   mild curry paste   15 ml
2 tsp   turmeric   10 ml
1 oz   wholemeal flour   25 g
8 fl oz   semi-skimmed milk   240 ml
4 fl oz   natural yogurt   115 ml
4 tbsp   single cream   60 ml

Separate the broccoli into stalks and florets; cook the stalks until tender, then chop finely. Halve the eggs, sieve the yolks and mix with the chopped broccoli stalks, chutney and seasoning. Pipe the mixture into the egg halves, retaining two egg white halves for garnish.

Melt the margarine, add the onions and cook until soft. Add the curry paste and turmeric and cook for 2 minutes. Stir in the flour and cook gently for 1–2 minutes. Gradually add the milk and stir the sauce over the heat until thickened. Allow to cook, then remove from the heat, stir in the yogurt, cream and seasoning and process to obtain a smooth sauce.

Meanwhile, cook the broccoli florets until just tender; drain. Arrange the eggs and broccoli in a serving dish and spoon the sauce over the eggs.

Garnish sliced egg white; almonds; redcurrants; fresh thyme

Protein – high
Fat – high
Fibre – medium

Potato Medley

4 × 6–8-oz   potatoes   4 × 175–225 g

Scrub the potatoes well, prick with a fork and bake for about 1 hour at 375°F/190°C/gas mark 5 until soft.

Suggested fillings (for 1 serving)

Pesto: Scoop out the potato flesh, mash with 1 tsp/5 ml pesto sauce and a little margarine and replace in the potato skin. Mix together 1 tsp/5 ml Parmesan cheese with 1 tsp/5 ml chopped mixed nuts, sprinkle over the potato and brown under the grill.

Nutty Cream: Blend together 2 tsp/10 ml soured cream, ½ oz/10 g Roquefort cheese, 1 tsp/5 ml chopped walnuts and a few snipped chives. Scoop out the potato flesh, mash with the cream mixture and replace in the potato skin. Garnish with a walnut half.

Chinese Mushrooms: Scoop out the potato flesh and mash lightly. Stir-fry ½ oz/10 g sliced mushrooms with a dash of soy sauce and place in the potato skin. Top with piped potato and a slice of Mozzarella cheese and brown under the grill.

Guacamole: Scoop out the potato flesh, mash with quarter of an avocado, a little margarine, a little cooked crushed garlic (optional), a dash of lemon juice and seasoning. Pipe into the potato skin.

Garnish tomato; Chinese leaf; fresh thyme; sliced spring onion

Analysis for Potato only:

Protein – low
Fat – low
Fibre – medium

Dhal

2 tbsp	polyunsaturated oil 30 ml
8 oz	onions, thinly sliced 225 g
1 tsp	cumin seeds 5 ml
	1 clove garlic, finely chopped
1 tsp	ground coriander 5 ml
8 oz	lentils 225 g
1 tsp	ground cinnamon 5 ml
	pinch ground cloves
1½ pints	vegetable stock 900 ml
	1 fresh bay leaf
	salt and freshly ground pepper

Soak the lentils as required (see page 4). Drain, rinse and put in a pan of cold water. Bring to the boil and cook rapidly for 10 minutes. Drain.

Heat the oil and sauté the onion, cumin seeds and garlic until the onion is soft. Add the coriander and cook for a further 2–3 minutes.

Stir in the lentils, cinnamon and cloves and cook for 1 minute, stirring constantly. Add the stock, bay leaf and seasoning and bring to the boil. Simmer for 45 minutes, remove the bay leaf before serving.

Serve with rice or naan bread, accompanied by side dishes such as chutney, fried banana and grated coconut, or serve the dhal as an accompaniment to vegetable curry.

Garnish spring onion fleuron; sliced radish; fresh basil

Protein – medium
Fat – medium
Fibre – high

Nutty Hotpot with Cheese Dumplings

1 tbsp	polyunsaturated oil	15 ml
4 oz	onions, cut into wedges	100 g
4 oz	cauliflower, broken into florets	100 g
3 oz	peas, fresh or frozen	75 g
2 oz	green beans	50 g
4 oz	canned tomatoes, chopped	100 g
2 oz	courgettes, sliced	50 g
4 oz	roasted peanuts, unsalted	100 g
1 tsp	chopped fresh mixed herbs (oregano, thyme, basil and chives)	5 ml
1 tsp	yeast extract	5 ml
	mixed with	
¾ pint	boiling water	450 ml

Cheese Dumplings

4 oz	self-raising wholemeal flour	100 g
2 oz	polyunsaturated margarine	50 g
1 oz	low-fat Cheddar cheese, grated	25 g
	cold water to bind	
1 oz	rolled oats	25 g

Heat the oil and sauté the onion until soft. Stir in the remaining hotpot ingredients and season well. Cover and simmer for 15 minutes.

Meanwhile, make the dumplings. Sieve the flour and rub in the margarine. Mix in the cheese and season well. Add sufficient water to make a soft dough, form into balls and roll lightly in the oats.

Put the hotpot mixture in one large or four individual casseroles. Top with the dumplings and bake at 375°F/190°C/gas mark 5 for 30–40 minutes, until the dumplings are cooked.

Variation
Experiment with seasonal vegetables.

Garnish paprika; chicory; lollorosso

Protein – medium	
Fat – high	
Fibre – high	

The
WINTER
collection

Twenty delicious dishes without meat

Vegetable Tortilla

2 tbsp	polyunsaturated oil 30 ml
6 oz	onions, sliced 175 g
6 oz	carrots, canelled and sliced 175 g
12 oz	white cabbage, sliced 350 g
12 oz	courgettes, canelled and sliced 350 g
½ pint	vegetable stock 300 ml
¼ pint	tomato juice 150 ml
2 tbsp	tomato purée 30 ml
1 tbsp	paprika 15 ml
1 tsp	chopped fresh mixed herbs (chives, oregano, basil and thyme) 5 ml
1 tsp	caraway seeds 5 ml
	pinch ground nutmeg
	salt and freshly ground pepper
2 tbsp	natural yogurt 30 ml
2 tbsp	single cream 30 ml
3 oz	tortilla chips 75 g

Heat the oil and sauté the onion until soft. Add the carrots, cabbage and courgettes and cook for a further 5 minutes. Mix thoroughly. Stir in all the other ingredients except for the yogurt and cream and simmer for 15–20 minutes.

Transfer the mixture to a serving dish. Mix the yogurt and cream together and pour in a line down the centre of the dish.

Serve with tortilla chips.

Variation
Serve with brown rice, noodles, couscous or pitta bread instead of the tortilla chips.

Garnish chopped fresh parsley; shredded cabbage; sliced carrots; sliced courgettes; spring onion tops cut in diamonds

Protein – low
Fat – medium
Fibre – medium

Lemon and Millet Hotpot

4 oz	millet 100 g
3 oz	polyunsaturated margarine 75 g
3 oz	onions, diced 75 g
6 oz	leeks, sliced 175 g
4 oz	carrots, grated 100 g
4 oz	courgettes, diced 100 g
1 stick celery, diced	
1 oz	flour 25 g
½ pint	semi-skimmed milk 300 ml
1 tsp	chopped fresh parsley 5 ml
1 tsp	chopped fresh sage 5 ml
grated rind and juice of 1 lemon	
salt and freshly ground pepper	
3 oz	low-fat soft cheese, diced 75 g

Cook the millet in boiling water. Melt 2 oz/50 g of the margarine and sauté the onion, leeks, carrots, courgettes and celery for 10–15 minutes. Add the millet and keep hot.

Meanwhile, melt the remaining margarine, add the flour and cook gently for a few minutes. Add the milk gradually and heat, stirring constantly, to make a smooth sauce. Allow to cook, then stir in the herbs, lemon rind and juice and simmer for 2 minutes. Season. Add 2 oz/50 g of the soft cheese and stir over a gentle heat until smooth, do not allow to boil. Add the vegetables and millet and mix well. Transfer to a serving dish, top with the remaining cheese and brown under the grill.

Variation
Experiment with seasonal vegetables.

Garnish potato crisps; diced red pepper; mustard and cress; fresh rosemary

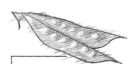

Protein – low
Fat – high
Fibre – medium

Lentil Pilaf

1 tbsp	polyunsaturated oil 15 ml
4 oz	onions, sliced 100 g
6 oz	lentils 175 g
8 oz	brown rice 225 g
2 oz	carrots, grated 50 g
1 tsp	ground cinnamon 5 ml
1 tsp	ground cloves 5 ml
1 tsp	fennel seeds 5 ml
	salt and freshly ground pepper
1 pint	vegetable stock 600 ml
3 oz	raisins 75 g
2 oz	walnuts, chopped 50 g

Soak lentils as required (see page 4). Drain, rinse and put in a pan of cold water. Bring to the boil and cook rapidly for 10 minutes. Drain.

Heat the oil and sauté the onion. Stir in the lentils, rice and carrots. Add the cinnamon, cloves, fennel seeds and seasoning and stir over a moderate heat for 2–3 minutes. Add the stock and bring to the boil. Cover, reduce the heat and simmer until the stock is absorbed (about 30 minutes). Stir the mixture to check consistency, adding more water if required. Add the raisins and nuts. Cover and simmer very gently for a further 10 minutes.

For attractive presentation, press the mixture into a small pudding mould and turn out on to a serving dish. Serve with natural yogurt laced with curry sauce (see page 97).

Variations
Use the pilaf as a stuffing for vegetables, such as marrow or peppers, or serve as an accompaniment to another dish.

Replace walnuts with cashews or whole peanuts.

Garnish spring onion; Chinese leaves; raspberries; snipped fresh chives

Protein – high
Fat – medium
Fibre – high

Camembert Croquettes

8 oz	fairly firm Camembert cheese 225 g
2 tbsp	wholemeal flour 30 ml
½ tsp	dry mustard 2.5 ml
½ tsp	chopped, fresh mixed herbs 2.5 ml
	salt and freshly ground pepper
	1 egg, beaten
2 oz	wholemeal breadcrumbs 50 g
½ tsp	chilli powder 2.5 ml
	pinch cayenne pepper
	polyunsaturated oil for frying
4 tbsp	natural yogurt 60 ml

Divide the cheese into 8 portions, wrap in cling film and freeze for 1 hour.

Mix the flour, mustard, herbs and seasoning together, then mix the breadcrumbs with the chilli powder and cayenne. Dip the cheese portions first into the flour mixture, then in the beaten egg and finally the breadcrumb mixture. Deep-fry the cheese in the oil for about 30 seconds until golden-brown. Drain and serve with a crisp salad and natural yogurt.

Variations
Substitute Brie, Chèvre or Ricotta cheese for the Camembert and vary the coating by mixing oatmeal with breadcrumbs.

Serve this dish more traditionally with a cranberry sauce or redcurrant purée.

Garnish natural yogurt; Chinese leaves; lollorosso; cherry tomato; red chilli; sliced spring onion

Protein – high
Fat – high
Fibre – low

Vegetable Fusilli

1 oz polyunsaturated margarine 25 g
1 oz flour 25 g
½ pint semi-skimmed milk 300 ml
4 oz low-fat Cheddar cheese, grated 100 g
pinch ground nutmeg
salt and freshly ground pepper
2 oz mushrooms, sliced 50 g
2 oz mixed sweet peppers, diced 50 g
2 oz celery, thinly sliced 50 g
2 oz courgettes, thinly sliced 50 g
8 oz wholewheat, egg or spinach fusilli 225 g
1 oz peas, fresh or frozen 25 g
1 oz Parmesan cheese, grated 25 g

Melt the margarine, add the flour and cook gently for 1–2 minutes. Add the milk gradually and heat, stirring constantly, to obtain a smooth texture. Allow the sauce to cook, then add the grated Cheddar cheese, nutmeg and seasoning.

Sauté the mushrooms, peppers, celery and courgettes lightly, retaining some raw vegetables for the garnish.

Boil the pasta until just cooked. Drain and refresh.

Combine the cooked vegetables, cheese sauce and pasta with the peas. Turn into an ovenproof dish, sprinkle with Parmesan and bake at 375°F/190°C/gas mark 5 for about 20 minutes, until light brown and bubbling.

Variations
Use different colours and shapes of pasta.

Try different seasonal vegetables.

Garnish blanched vegetables; sprig of fresh basil

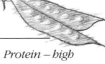

Protein – high
Fat – medium
Fibre – high

Spinach Roulade

1 lb spinach, chopped 450 g
1 bunch watercress, chopped
1 tsp chopped fresh sage 5 ml
pinch ground nutmeg
1 oz polyunsaturated margarine 25 g
1 oz flour 25 g
½ pint semi-skimmed milk 300 ml
2 eggs, separated
salt and freshly ground pepper
6 oz cream cheese, softened 175 g
8 oz filo pastry 225 g
1 egg
2 tbsp semi-skimmed milk 30 ml

Cook and refresh the spinach. Blend with the watercress, sage and nutmeg in a food processor until smooth.

Melt the margarine, add the flour and cook gently for 1–2 minutes. Gradually add the milk and heat, stirring constantly, to make a smooth sauce. Allow the sauce to cook, then cool slightly, then add the 2 egg yolks and the spinach mixture to the sauce. Mix thoroughly.

Whisk the 2 egg whites to fairly stiff peaks and fold into the sauce. Season. Pour the mixture into a greased and lined Swiss roll tin and bake at 350°F/180°C/gas mark 4 for about 20 minutes. Turn out on to greaseproof paper sprinkled lightly with flour and allow to cool. Spread with the cream cheese and roll up like a Swiss roll.

Lay one sheet of filo pastry on a clean work surface and brush with cold water. Place a second layer on top and brush with water. Brush all the edges with water and wrap roulade in the pastry, sealing the edges. Combine the egg and milk and egg wash the pastry. Place the roulade on a greased tray and bake at 400°F/200°C/gas mark 6 until crisp and golden-brown.

Variations
Spread the roulade with a stuffing before rolling such as an apricot and nut combination.

Serve the roulade without the pastry cover.

Garnish kiwi fruit slices; baby sweetcorn; fresh basil; tomato sauce (see page 96)

Protein – high
Fat – high
Fibre – low

Winter Cobbler

Filling

8 oz   aubergines, sliced   225 g
4 oz   onions, chopped   100 g
4 oz   carrots, sliced   100 g
6 oz   courgettes, sliced   175 g
4 oz   cauliflower, broken into florets   100 g
8 oz   canned tomatoes, chopped   225 g
1 clove garlic, finely chopped
2 tbsp   tomato purée   30 ml
dash Tabasco
dash Worcestershire sauce
½ pint   vegetable stock   300 ml
salt and freshly ground pepper

Topping

4 oz   wholemeal flour   100 g
4 oz   plain flour   100 g
2 tsp   baking powder   10 ml
4 oz   polyunsaturated margarine   100 g
8 fl oz   semi-skimmed milk   240 ml

Sprinkle the aubergine slices with salt and leave to drain for 30 minutes, then rinse and dry thoroughly. Carefully combine all the ingredients for the filling in a saucepan, reserving some vegetables for garnish, bring to the boil and simmer for 15 minutes.

To prepare the topping, combine the flours and baking powder, rub in the margarine and add sufficient milk to form a dough. Roll out the dough to a thickness of 1 in/2.5 cm and cut into four circles 2¼ in/6 cm in diameter.

Put the vegetable mixture in an ovenproof dish and top with the scone circles. Bake at 350°F/180°C/gas mark 4 for 20–25 minutes, until the scones are well risen and brown. The colour can be enhanced by putting under the grill for a few minutes.

Variations

Boost the protein content by adding cooked lentils to the filling before baking.

For ease of preparation use a savoury scone mix for the topping.

Garnish blanched cauliflower florets; courgette and carrot slices; chopped fresh parsley

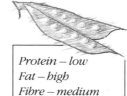

Protein – low
Fat – high
Fibre – medium

Wholemeal Lentil Pancakes

8 pancakes, made with wholemeal flour (see page 16)

Filling

2 oz	polyunsaturated margarine	50 g
2 tsp	polyunsaturated oil	10 ml
3 oz	onions, finely chopped	75 g
8 oz	lentils	225 g
½ pint	vegetable stock	300 ml
8 oz	canned tomatoes, chopped	225 g
1 tsp	ground coriander	5 ml
1 tsp	tomato purée	5 ml
½ tsp	soft brown sugar	2.5 ml
2 tbsp	red wine (optional)	30 ml
5 oz	mushrooms, sliced	150 g

Parsley Sauce

1 oz	polyunsaturated margarine	25 g
1 oz	flour	25 g
½ pint	semi-skimmed milk	300 ml
4 tbsp	natural yogurt	60 ml
2 tsp	chopped fresh parsley	10 ml
½ tsp	lemon juice	2.5 ml
	salt and freshly ground pepper	

Soak the lentils as required (see page 4). Drain, rinse and put in a pan of cold water. Bring to the boil and cook rapidly for 10 minutes. Drain.

To make the filling, heat the margarine and oil together and sauté the onion until soft. Add the lentils, stock, tomatoes, coriander, tomato purée, sugar and wine and simmer gently, uncovered, for about 30 minutes. Add the mushrooms and cook for 5 minutes.

To make the sauce, melt the margarine, add the flour and cook for 1–2 minutes. Add the milk gradually and stir over a gentle heat to make a smooth sauce. Add the remaining ingredients and cook gently for a few minutes.

Fill each pancake with the lentil mixture, roll or fold and arrange in a dish. Coat with parsley sauce and serve piping hot.

Garnish diced red pepper; sliced kiwi fruit; lollorosso; chicory leaves; fresh thyme

Protein – high
Fat – high
Fibre – high

Cashew and Mushroom Loaf

1 tbsp   polyunsaturated oil   15 ml
3 oz   onions, finely chopped   75 g
1 clove garlic, finely chopped
5 oz   cashew nuts   150 g
3 oz   fresh wholemeal breadcrumbs   75 g
1 egg, beaten
2 medium parsnips, cooked and mashed
1 tsp   fresh rosemary, chopped   5 ml
1 tsp   fresh thyme, chopped   5 ml
1 tsp   yeast extract   5 ml
¼ pint   vegetable stock   150 ml
salt and freshly ground pepper
½ oz   polyunsaturated margarine   10 g
5 oz   mushrooms, sliced   150 g

Heat the oil and sauté the onion and garlic until soft. Grind the cashew nuts in a blender and mix with the breadcrumbs. Add the egg and mix in the mashed parsnips and herbs. Add the onion and garlic. Dissolve the yeast extract in the hot stock and add to the other ingredients. Season well. Adjust consistency with stock or breadcrumbs. Melt the margarine and sauté the mushrooms.

Grease a 1-lb/450-g loaf tin and press in half the nut mixture, then cover with a layer of mushrooms and top with the rest of the nut mixture. Cover with foil and bake at 350°F/180°C/gas mark 4 for 1 hour. Leave to stand for 10 minutes, then turn out. The loaf may be served hot or cold.

Variations

Use wild mushrooms for an unusual but more expensive combination.

Substitute asparagus for the mushrooms.

Garnish dressing made by combining natural yogurt with a little tomato purée and honey to flavour; lollorosso; turned mushrooms; celery tops; Chinese leaves; mustard and cress

Protein – low
Fat – high
Fibre – low

Chinese Vegetables with Pasta

8 oz	wholewheat noodles or tagliatelle 225 g
4 oz	carrots, canelled and sliced 100 g
4 oz	turnips, cut in julienne strips 100 g
4 oz	mooli, canelled and sliced 100 g
4 oz	celery, sliced at an angle 100 g
4 oz	red and green peppers, cut in diamonds 100 g
2 oz	whole French beans, cut in 1-inch/2.5-cm lengths 50 g
2 oz	beansprouts 50 g
¼ pint	pineapple juice 150 ml
2 tbsp	soy sauce 30 ml
	small piece of fresh ginger, peeled and chopped
	salt and freshly ground pepper
2 tbsp	polyunsaturated oil 30 ml
1 oz	polyunsaturated margarine 25 g
4 oz	mushrooms, sliced 100 g

Cook the noodles in boiling, salted water until just cooked. Drain and refresh. Blanch the carrots, turnips, mooli, celery, peppers and French beans in boiling water for 4 minutes. Refresh and drain. Retain some vegetables for garnish. Rinse and drain the beansprouts. Blend the pineapple juice with ¼ pint/150 ml cold water, the ginger, soy sauce and seasoning. Set aside.

Heat the oil and margarine together in a large pan or wok and stir-fry all the vegetables, except the mushrooms and beansprouts, for 3 minutes. Add the pineapple juice mixture and stir-fry for a further 5 minutes. Stir in the noodles, mushrooms and beansprouts and fry for 2 minutes. Serve immediately.

Variation
Increase the protein content by adding cooked lentils to the mixture.

Garnish blanched vegetables; fresh basil

Protein – low
Fat – medium
Fibre – high

Walnut and Roquefort Savoury

1 oz	polyunsaturated margarine 25 g
2 oz	onions, finely chopped 50 g
10 oz	potatoes 275 g
2 tsp	chopped fresh parsley 10 ml
1 tbsp	skimmed milk powder 15 ml
	pinch ground nutmeg
	salt and freshly ground pepper
	3 egg whites, stiffly beaten
8 oz	blue cheese (Stilton, Roquefort or Danish Blue) 225 g
4 oz	cottage cheese 100 g
	3 egg yolks
¼ pint	natural yogurt 150 ml
3 oz	walnuts, halved 75 g

Melt the margarine and sauté the onions until soft; drain off the margarine and reserve. Boil and drain the potatoes, reserving the cooking water. Mash the potatoes and stir in the onion and parsley. Add the margarine, milk powder, nutmeg and seasoning and enough of the potato water to make a light mash. Beat the mixture well. Fold in the egg whites carefully and put the mixture in a well-greased dish.

Sieve the cheeses together, add the egg yolks and yogurt and mix thoroughly. Pour this mixture over the potatoes and garnish with the walnut halves.

Bake at 350°F/180°C/gas mark 4 for 30 minutes until the top is golden-brown. Serve accompanied by a crisp salad.

Garnish sliced strawberry; fresh thyme; sliced mooli; walnut halves

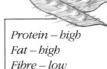

Protein – high
Fat – high
Fibre – low

Chilli Beans

5 oz dried mixed beans 150 g	
(borlotti, cannellini and haricot, shown in the photograph)	
1 tbsp polyunsaturated oil 15 ml	
4 oz onions, chopped 100 g	
Chilli Sauce	
1 oz soft brown sugar 25 g	
2 tbsp soy sauce 30 ml	
2 tbsp wine vinegar 30 ml	
1 tsp tomato purée 5 ml	
1 tsp dry mustard 5 ml	
½ tsp chilli powder 2.5 ml	
1 tsp paprika 5 ml	
½ pint vegetable stock 300 ml	
3 oz red peppers, sliced 75 g	
1 tsp potato flour (fecule) 5 ml	

Soak the beans overnight (see page 3). Drain, rinse and put in separate pans of cold water. Bring to the boil and cook rapidly for 10 minutes. Reduce the heat and simmer for required time. Drain. Alternatively use 1 lb/450 g canned or cooked mixed beans.

Heat the oil and sauté the onion until soft. Combine all the sauce ingredients except the stock, peppers and potato flour and add to the onion. Cook for 5 minutes, then add the stock, red peppers and beans. Bring to the boil and simmer for 10 minutes.

Blend the potato flour with a little cold water, add to the mixture and stir until thickened. Serve with brown and wild rice or wholewheat pasta.

Garnish red chillis; diced cucumber;
diced radish; sliced spring onion

Protein – low
Fat – low
Fibre – high

Cheese and Vegetable Macaroni

6 oz short-cut wholewheat or egg macaroni 175 g	
2 oz polyunsaturated margarine 50 g	
12 oz leeks, chopped 350 g	
2 oz flour 50 g	
1½ pints semi-skimmed milk 900 ml	
8 oz low-fat Cheddar cheese, grated 225 g	
salt and freshly ground pepper	
2 oz wholemeal breadcrumbs 50 g	
1 tsp snipped fresh chives 5 ml	

Cook the macaroni until just tender. Drain well and refresh. Melt the margarine and sauté the leeks for 2 minutes. Stir in the flour and cook for a minute. Gradually stir in the milk and heat, stirring constantly, to make a smooth sauce. Add 6 oz/175 g of the cheese and all the macaroni and season well.

Spoon the mixture into an ovenproof dish. Combine the breadcrumbs, chives and remaining cheese and sprinkle evenly across the top of the dish. Bake at 375°F/190°C/gas mark 5 for 30–35 minutes, until golden-brown.

Variations
Try other seasonal vegetables.

Use pasta shapes instead of macaroni.

Mix sesame seeds with the cheese topping to vary the flavour.

Garnish julienne of leeks, blanched

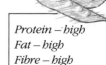

Protein – high
Fat – high
Fibre – high

Lentil Pasties

8 oz   swede, diced   225 g
6 oz   lentils   175 g
1 pint   vegetable stock   600 ml
1 fresh bay leaf
salt and freshly ground pepper
1 oz   polyunsaturated margarine   25 g
3 oz   onions, finely chopped   75 g
2 tsp   chopped fresh mixed herbs (basil, chives, oregano and thyme)   10 ml
1 tbsp   tomato purée   15 ml
8 oz   puff pastry   225 g
4 oz   Mozzarella cheese   100 g
1 egg
2 tbsp   semi-skimmed milk   30 ml

Soak lentils as required (see page 4). Drain, rinse and put in a pan of cold water. Bring to the boil and cook rapidly for 10 minutes. Drain.

Cook, drain and mash the swede. Meanwhile, put the lentils, stock, bay leaf and seasoning in a pan and simmer for 30 minutes until the lentils are tender. Drain if necessary and remove the bay leaf. Melt the margarine and sauté the onion until golden. Mix in the swede and lentils and add the herbs and tomato purée.

Roll out the pastry and cut into four 6-in/15-cm diameter circles. Spoon a portion of the lentil mixture on to half of each circle. Brush the pastry edges with water, then fold over and press the edges together firmly to seal. Place the pasties on an oiled baking tray. Mix the egg and milk, and use to brush the pasties. Top with Mozzarella slices and bakc at 425°F/170°C/gas mark 3 for 15 minutes.

Serve with lentil Béchamel (see page 96).

Garnish endive; fresh flat-leaf parsley; paprika

Protein – high
Fat – high
Fibre – high

Vegetable Symphony

1 medium cauliflower, broken into florets
1 lb   courgettes, canelled and sliced   450 g
4 oz   mushrooms, sliced   100 g
2 oz   polyunsaturated margarine   50 g
1 oz   flour   25 g
½ pint   semi-skimmed milk   300 ml
salt and freshly ground pepper
4 oz   low-fat soft cheese   100 g
1 tbsp   wholemeal breadcrumbs   15 ml
½ oz   pine kernels   10 g
1 tsp   snipped fresh chives   5 ml

Cook the cauliflower and courgettes in separate pans of boiling water until just tender; drain. Meanwhile, cook the mushrooms in half the margarine for 3–4 minutes; drain.

Layer half the courgettes, all the cauliflower and all the mushrooms in an ovenproof dish; top with remaining courgettes. Melt the remaining margarine, add the flour and cook for 1–2 minutes. Stir in the milk and continue stirring until the sauce thickens. Allow to cook, then season and add the cheese. Pour the sauce over the vegetables and sprinkle the top with breadcrumbs. Place under the grill until lightly browned. Sprinkle with pine kernels and snipped chives before serving.

Serve accompanied by a tomato sauce (see page 96).

Garnish kiwi fruit; lollorosso; mustard
and cress

Protein – low
Fat – medium
Fibre – low

Midwinter Pie

2 lb	potatoes, cooked 900 g
¼ pint	semi-skimmed milk 150 ml
1 oz	polyunsaturated margarine 25 g
	pinch ground nutmeg
	1 egg
8 oz	onions, sliced 225 g
8 oz	fresh broccoli 225 g
2 oz	wholemeal breadcrumbs 50 g
1 tsp	chopped fresh rosemary 5 ml
1 tsp	chopped fresh parsley 5 ml
1 tsp	chopped fresh basil 5 ml
2 oz	Parmesan cheese, grated 50 g
	salt and freshly ground pepper
4 oz	low-fat Cheddar cheese, grated 100 g

Cream half the potatoes with the milk, margarine, nutmeg and egg or, as an alternative, separate the eggs, add the yolks to the potato mixture, then whip the whites stiffly and fold into the potato purée. Cut the remaining potatoes into slices. Sauté the onions in a little margarine but do not allow to turn brown.

Steam or boil the broccoli until tender but still crisp. Meanwhile, mix the breadcrumbs, herbs, Parmesan and seasoning. Place the sliced potatoes in the base of an oiled casserole, followed by the onions, Cheddar cheese and broccoli. Top with the creamed potato mixture and sprinkle with the breadcrumb mixture. Bake at 375°F/190°C/gas mark 5 for about 15 minutes until lightly browned.

Serve accompanied by Béchamel and yogurt sauce (see page 96).

Variation
Replace the broccoli with another vegetable, such as leek or cauliflower.

Garnish sliced strawberry; watercress

Protein – high
Fat – medium
Fibre – high

Nutty Vegetable Flan

8 oz	wholemeal pastry 225 g
6 oz	cauliflower, broken into small florets 175 g
3 oz	carrots, chopped 75 g
3 oz	green beans, diced 75 g
½	green pepper, diced
2 oz	roasted peanuts 50 g
	2 eggs
½ pint	semi-skimmed milk 300 ml
2 oz	Edam cheese, grated 50 g
	salt and freshly ground pepper

Line 1 large or 4 small flan dishes with the pastry and bake blind (see page 102).

Blanch all the vegetables, refresh and divide between the pastry cases. Roughly chop the peanuts and sprinkle evenly over the vegetables. Beat the eggs and milk together. Mix in the cheese, season and pour the mixture over the vegetables.

Bake the flan at 350°F/180°C/gas mark 4 for about 25 minutes, until the filling is set. Serve hot or cold accompanied by tomato sauce (see page 96).

Variation
Experiment with different vegetables and nuts.

Garnish chicory leaves; spring onion fleuron; fresh mint leaf; celery top; sliced radish; baby sweetcorn

Protein – high
Fat – high
Fibre – high

Fresh Herb Oatcakes

1 tbsp	polyunsaturated oil 15 ml
4 oz	onions, finely chopped 100 g
5 oz	low-fat Cheddar cheese, finely grated 150 g
4 oz	wholemeal breadcrumbs 100 g
½ tsp	chopped fresh thyme 2.5 ml
½ tsp	chopped fresh rosemary 2.5 ml
½ tsp	chopped fresh sage 2.5 ml
	pinch ground nutmeg
	pinch dry mustard
	salt and freshly ground pepper
	1 egg, beaten
	1 egg
2 tbsp	semi-skimmed milk 30 ml
1 oz	rolled oats 25 g

Heat the oil and sauté the onion until soft. Allow to cool. Mix the onion with the cheese, breadcrumbs, herbs, nutmeg, mustard and seasonings. Combine with the beaten egg. Shape the mixture into balls. Whisk the egg and milk lightly. Dip the balls in the egg wash and coat in the rolled oats. Shallow-fry to seal and colour and then bake at 425°F/220°C/gas mark 7 for 15–20 minutes.

Serve with a dip, such as garlic mayonnaise, or to make a more substantial dish, serve with wholewheat spaghetti in a curry sauce (see page 97), as shown.

Garnish fresh mint leaves; spring onion fleurons

Protein – high
Fat – medium
Fibre – low

Indonesian-style Vegetables

2 tbsp   polyunsaturated oil   30 ml
4 oz   onions, chopped   100 g
1 clove garlic, finely chopped
½ tsp   turmeric   2.5 ml
½ tsp   paprika   2.5 ml
½ tsp   ground cumin   2.5 ml
½ tsp   dry mustard   2.5 ml
2 tbsp   tomato purée   30 ml
½ vegetable stock cube
1 lb   potatoes, cut into 1-in/2.5-cm cubes   450 g
1 cauliflower, broken into florets
¾ pint   water   450 ml
salt and freshly ground pepper
small piece fresh ginger, peeled and finely chopped
¼ pint   natural yogurt   150 ml
½ tsp   chopped fresh coriander   2.5 ml
½ tsp   chopped fresh mint   2.5 ml

Heat the oil and sauté the onion and garlic until soft. Add the spices and stir well. Stir in the tomato purée and the crumbled stock cube. Add the potatoes and cauliflower, stirring well so that the flavours penetrate the vegetables. Pour on the water and add the seasoning and ginger. Bring to the boil and simmer for 15–20 minutes, until all the vegetables are just cooked.

Strain off a little of the cooking liquid into a bowl and blend in the yogurt. Stir this mixture into the vegetables. Mix well, sprinkle with the chopped herbs and serve with wholewheat pasta shells, macaroni or brown rice.

Variation
To increase the protein content, add sliced hard-boiled eggs or cooked chickpeas.

Garnish fresh oregano leaves; natural yogurt

Protein – low
Fat – medium
Fibre – medium

Beanfeast

5 oz	dried mixed beans	150 g
1½ oz	dried green split peas	40 g
2 oz	polyunsaturated margarine	50 g
1 tbsp	polyunsaturated oil	15 ml
	2 leeks, chopped	
	2 carrots, chopped	
	2 sticks celery, chopped	
	1 onion, sliced	
	2 courgettes, sliced	
4 oz	canned tomatoes, chopped	100 g
2 oz	mushrooms, sliced	50 g
1 tbsp	fine oatmeal	15 ml
2 tbsp	tomato purée	30 ml
1¼ pints	vegetable stock	750 ml
2 tsp	yeast extract	10 ml
½ tsp	ground mace	2.5 ml
½ tsp	chopped fresh mint	2.5 ml
½ tsp	ground coriander	2.5 ml
1 tsp	chopped fresh parsley	5 ml
1 tsp	chopped fresh thyme	5 ml

Parsley Dumplings

2 oz	polyunsaturated margarine	50 g
4 oz	self-raising wholemeal flour	100 g
2 tsp	chopped fresh parsley	10 ml
	cold water to bind	

Soak the beans and peas overnight (see page 3). Drain, put in separate pans of cold water. Bring to the boil and cook rapidly for 10 minutes. Reduce heat and simmer for required time. Drain. Alternatively use 1 lb/450 g canned or cooked mixed beans and 4 oz/100 g canned or cooked green split peas.

Heat the margarine and oil together and sauté the vegetables for 15 minutes. Stir in the oatmeal and cook for 1 minute, then add all the other ingredients except the yeast extract, mace and herbs and cook for a further 20 minutes.

To make the dumplings: rub the margarine into the flour, then add the parsley and enough water to mix to a soft dough. Divide the dough into four dumplings, and steam, covered, over a pan of boiling water for 15 minutes. Add the yeast extract, mace and herbs to the bean mixture. Place the dumplings on top and simmer, covered for about 20 minutes.

Garnish chopped spring onion; fresh thyme

Protein – high
Fat – high
Fibre – high

Sauces, Garnishes and Sandwiches

Sauce Recipes

These appetizing sauces have been adapted to reflect the trend for healthy eating. Provided the ingredients are used in the given quantities each sauce contains less fat than in the traditional recipe. They can be served with any appropriate dish in addition to the suggestions made in the seasonal recipes.

White Béchamel Sauce
Makes about 1 pint/600 ml

2 oz   polyunsaturated margarine   50 g
2 oz   flour   50 g
1 pint   semi-skimmed milk   600 ml
1 onion clouté (see page 102)

Heat the milk with the onion until just below boiling point. Remove from the heat and allow to stand for 15 minutes.

Melt the margarine, stir in the flour and cook for a few minutes over a gentle heat without allowing the roux to colour. Remove from the heat and allow to cool.

Strain the milk and add to the roux gradually to make a smooth sauce. Heat, stirring until smooth, replace the onion and allow to cook.

Remove the onion, season to taste and strain if necessary.

Variations
YOGURT   Replace 4 fl oz/115 ml of the semi-skimmed milk with natural yogurt adding it when the sauce has been made. Do not allow the sauce to boil after adding the yogurt.

CHEESE   Add 2 oz/50 g grated low-fat Cheddar cheese, to the Béchamel sauce, remove from the heat and do not allow to boil.

ONION   Sauté 4 oz/100 g chopped or diced onions in polyunsaturated margarine until soft but without allowing them to turn colour. Add to the Béchamel sauce.

MUSHROOM   Sauté 4 oz/100 g well washed, sliced white button mushrooms without allowing them to turn colour, add to the sauce and simmer for 10 minutes.

SPINACH   Process the Béchamel sauce with 4 oz/100 g cooked chopped spinach flavoured with a pinch of nutmeg.

LENTIL   Add a purée of 2 oz/50 g lentils – soaked, cooked and drained – to the basic Béchamel sauce.

MINT   Add freshly chopped mint to the basic Béchamel sauce.

Tomato Sauce
Makes about ½ pint/300 ml

½ oz   polyunsaturated margarine   10 g
2 oz   onion, chopped   50 g
2 oz   carrot, chopped   50 g
1 oz   celery, chopped   25 g
½ bay leaf
sprig of thyme
½ oz   wholemeal flour   10 g
4 tbsp   tomato purée   60 ml
¾ pint   vegetable stock   450 ml
salt and freshly ground pepper

This is the traditional method for making tomato sauce.

Melt the margarine. Add the onion, carrot, celery, bay leaf and thyme, and brown slightly. Blend in the flour and cook to a sandy texture, allowing the mixture to colour slightly. Stir in the tomato purée and leave to cool. Add the boiling stock gradually and bring to the boil, stirring constantly. Season and allow to simmer for 1 hour.

Adjust the seasoning and either process or pass through a sieve.

'Quick' Tomato Sauce

Makes about ½ pint/300 ml

½ pint   vegetable stock   300 ml
1 oz   polyunsaturated margarine   25 g
2 oz   onion, finely chopped   50 g
15 oz   canned tomatoes, chopped   425 g
1 clove garlic, finely chopped
1 tbsp   tomato purée   15 ml
1 tsp   chopped fresh basil   5 ml
salt and freshly ground pepper

Melt the margarine and sauté the onion until soft. Add all the remaining ingredients, bring to the boil, stirring, then simmer, uncovered, for 20 minutes. Adjust the seasoning and either process or pass through a sieve.

Variation

Make a spicy tomato sauce by adding a few drops of Worcestershire sauce and a little chilli to taste.

Curry Sauce

Makes about ½ pint/300 ml

2 oz   onion, finely chopped   50 g
½ clove garlic, finely chopped
1 oz   polyunsaturated margarine   25 g
½ oz   wholemeal flour   10 g
2 tsp   curry powder   10 ml
2 tsp   tomato purée   10 ml
¾ pint   vegetable stock   450 ml
1 oz   apple, chopped   25 g
2 tsp   desiccated coconut   10 ml
1 tsp   sultanas   5 ml
1 tsp   chopped chutney   5 ml
2 tsp   ground ginger   10 ml
salt and freshly ground pepper

Melt the margarine and sauté the onion and garlic without allowing them to colour. Blend in the flour and curry powder and cook to a sandy texture. Stir in the tomato purée. Add the boiling stock gradually, stirring constantly to make a smooth sauce. Add the remaining ingredients and allow the sauce to simmer for 30 minutes. Adjust the seasoning.

For a smooth sauce, either process or pass through a sieve.

Barbecue Sauce

Makes about ½ pint/300 ml

1 tbsp	polyunsaturated oil 15 ml
2 oz	onion, finely chopped 50 g
1 clove garlic, finely chopped	
½ tsp	dry mustard 2.5 ml
1 tbsp	Worcestershire sauce 15 ml
2 tbsp	malt vinegar 30 ml
1 tbsp	tomato purée 15 ml
2 tbsp	light soft brown sugar 30 ml
½ tsp	chilli seasoning 2.5 ml
6 fl oz	vegetable stock 180 ml

Heat the oil and sauté the onion and garlic until soft. Stir in the mustard, Worcestershire sauce, vinegar, tomato purée, sugar, chilli seasoning and vegetable stock. Bring to the boil, cover and simmer for 7–8 minutes until slightly thickened.

Garnishes for Different Seasons

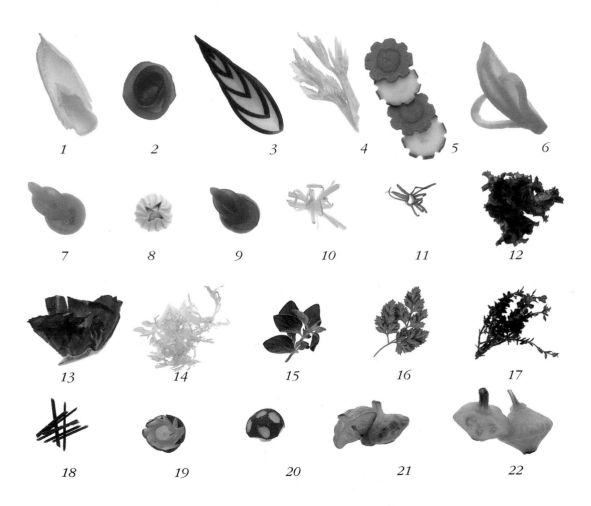

The garnishes shown in the photographs are only suggestions. They can be interchanged according to the season and availability.

1 Chicory
2 Tomato Rose
3 Feathered Apple
4 Celery Top
5 Canelled Carrot and Courgette
6 Kenley-style Lemon
7 Feathered Yellow Cherry Tomato
8 Turned Button Mushroom
9 Feathered Red Cherry Tomato
10 Spring Onion Fleuron
11 Spring Onion Top
12 Lollorosso
13 Radicchio
14 Spider Endive
15 Oregano
16 Dill
17 Thyme
18 Chives
19 Radish Rose
20 Toadstool Radish
21 Green Patty Pan Squash
22 Yellow Patty Pan Squash

Vegetarian Sandwiches

Types of Bread

Choose from the large range of breads that are now available to make imaginative sandwiches. Rolls and baps can also be used.

Wholewheat
Wheatgerm
Granary
Rye Bread
Oatcakes
Raisin Bread
Chapattis/Naan Bread
Malt Bread
Muffins
Sesame Bread

Wholemeal
Multi Grain
Soft Rye
Cheese Bread
Soda Bread
Pitta Bread/Tacos
Pumpernickel
French Bread
Croissants
Bagels

30 Suggestions for fillings

Cream cheese, diced celery and roasted peanuts

Grated cheese, beansprouts and dash of soy sauce

Honey, mashed banana and a sprinkling of desiccated coconut

Cottage cheese mixed with diced apricot on Chinese leaves

Dates cooked in lemon juice and water, mashed and chilled; spread thickly, top with cream cheese and chopped nuts

Edam cheese and sliced apples, topped with a fruit chutney

Sesame paste topped with beansprouts and sprinkled with sultanas

Peanut butter and yeast extract

Sliced avocado, topped with tomato, mayonnaise and a sprinkling of sunflower seeds

Cooked beans, lightly mashed with chicory leaves and sliced cucumber

Hummus, shredded lettuce and grated carrot

Thinly sliced nut roast and chutney

Diced Feta cheese and finely diced apple mixed with coleslaw

Chopped radish and red or green peppers mixed with cream cheese, topped with endive

Cold lentil dhal topped with tomato and a little yogurt dressing

Cottage cheese mixed with chopped avocado and cashew nuts

Mashed banana mixed with chopped dates and chopped mixed nuts

Chinese leaves topped with a potato and chive salad

Crunchy peanut butter topped with sliced banana and apple and sprinkled with lemon juice to preserve the colour

Yeast extract topped with cornflakes

Cream cheese topped with sliced mushrooms and beansprouts

Chopped Brie, mixed with diced apple, celery and cashew nuts – combine with a light yogurt dressing

Thinly sliced Stilton cheese topped with sliced pear and endive

Fromage frais topped with a muesli mixture and slices of apple

Cream cheese flavoured with pesto sauce topped with tomato slices

Sliced vegetable pâté topped with relish and shredded lettuce

Apricot jam, banana slices and flaked almonds

Shredded white cabbage, chopped red or green peppers and tomato in a soured cream dressing, piled on to a bed of watercress

Mushroom pâté spread with a wholegrain mustard

Chilled, cooked and puréed chickpeas, mixed with diced mixed red and green peppers, topped with Chinese leaves

Glossary of Terms

Definitions of some possibly unfamiliar terms used in the recipes in this book.

BAKE BLIND Put a sheet of greaseproof paper in the lined flan ring and fill with raw haricot beans. Bake at 400°F/200°C/gas mark 6 for about 15 minutes. Remove the beans and paper and put the flan in the oven for a further 10 minutes.

BECHAMEL A basic white sauce prepared by gradually adding heated milk to a white roux (cooked without allowing to colour). The sauce is stirred over a gentle heat until it thickens, then allowed to cook.

BLANCH Food (usually vegetables) is lowered into boiling water and quickly removed. Blanching helps to preserve colour and texture.

BUCKWHEAT FLOUR A strong flour with a distinctive flavour made from buckwheat grain. It is advisable to mix it with a white flour to lighten the texture.

BULGUR WHEAT Also known as cracked wheat. Soak for 30 minutes, drain and cover with two parts cold water to one of bulgur . Bring to the boil and simmer for 10–15 minutes. Serve hot as an accompaniment to pies or curries or cold with salads, as a substitute for rice.

CANELLE A knife with a special groove for channelling fruit or vegetables, see the garnishes on page 99 for an example.

COULIS A term for a smooth sauce or liquid purée which can be sweet (eg: raspberry) or savoury (eg: tomato).

COUSCOUS A cereal processed from semolina. It is usually steamed for about 1 hour. Serve as an accompaniment to main course dishes.

DARIOLE MOULD A rounded metal container with a flat base, about the size of a cup. Used for mousses and other mixtures which are turned out before serving.

MILLET Probably the first cereal grain to be used for domestic purposes. It is richer in vitamins, mineral and fat content than other grains. Use as an unusual alternative to rice.

OKRA A pod-like vegetable which can act as a thickening agent in some dishes. To prepare, wash and cut off the thick end. Okra can be deep-fried, microwaved, stewed, boiled or steamed.

ONION CLOUTE An onion studded with 4 cloves and one bay leaf. Infuse in milk to add flavour to sauces.

REFRESH Literally 'to cool down', the term is applied especially to cooked vegetables. They are immediately plunged into ice cold water to cool as quickly as possible.

RICOTTA A low-fat soft cheese made from whey that is suitable for vegetarians.

ROUX

A thickening element in sauces, made from equal quantities of flour and melted margarine. The mixture is stirred over a gentle heat to cook. The darker the required sauce, the longer the roux is cooked.

SESAME SEEDS

From the sesame plant, the seeds are rich in vitamins and minerals. Used to make tahini (sesame paste).

SPRING ONION FLEURON

Cut the top of a spring onion into thin strips to three-quarters of the length of the stem, leaving the base attached. Put in iced water until the strips have curled.

SWEAT

To cook in fat without allowing the food to turn colour. Term usually applied to vegetables.

TOFU

A pale-coloured, fermented soya bean curd of light texture, slightly thicker than cottage cheese. Delicious served with a well-flavoured sauce or dip.

WILD RICE

Quite different in taste from other types of rice, a traditional accompaniment to some classic dishes. Also effective mixed with long-grain rice to enhance its texture and appearance.

Index